39 65

Religious Freedom In America

by Charles C. Haynes

Published by the Americans United Research Foundation
in celebration of the Bicentennial Observances of the
UNITED STATES CONSTITUTION AND BILL OF RIGHTS

Acknowledgments

The Americans United Research Foundation gratefully acknowledges the following organization and individuals whose support made possible the publication of this book:

Dr. G. Richard Doerbaum

O.D. & Anna Ruth McKee

Mrs. Ebba E. Meyer

Scottish Rite Foundation
Southern Jurisdiction, U.S.A., Inc.

Mrs. Elin M. Winn

The author wishes to thank the staff of Americans United, particularly Dr. Robert L. Maddox, who first envisioned this project, Albert J. Menendez, who gave valuable advice, and Paula Wiley, who typed the manuscript with skill and made helpful suggestions along the way.

The process of identifying and reviewing classroom materials required help from many organizations and individuals. Special mention should be made of Wynell Burroughs of the National Archives, Minna Novick of the American Bar Association, Frances Sonnenschein of the Anti-Defamation League, Wes Bodin of the National Council on Religion and Public Education, and Tam Andrews, formerly of the Council for the Advancement of Citizenship.

Credits:

"The American Tradition of Religious Freedom: An Historical Analysis," by Robert T. Handy is reprinted from the *Journal of Public Law*, Vol. 13, No. 2 by permission of the *Emory Law Journal* (formerly the *Journal of Public Law*) of the Emory University School of Law.

"Teetering on the Wall of Separation," and "Pilgrimage to the Wall of Separation," by Isidore Starr are reprinted from *Update*, Winter, 1979 and Spring, 1985 by permission of the Special Committee of Youth Education for Citizenship of the American Bar Association.

Book design by Harry Knox

Library of Congress Catalog Card Number: 86-71632
ISBN 0-9617164-0-1

Contents

The Americans United Research Foundation, a non-partisan, non-sectarian organization committed to research in the area of church-state relations is pleased to present to America's teachers a guide for the teaching of religious liberty. We hope that high school social studies teachers will make use of this book to inform the nation's youth of the importance of religious freedom to our national heritage.

With the publication of this teachers' guide, several important tributaries of our work come together. The Americans United Research Foundation and its sister organization, Americans United for Separation of Church and State, have worked long and hard for the preservation of religious freedom. We believe in the power of education to broaden our understanding of each other. We have always insisted that the nation's public schools be free of government-sponsored religious activities while, at the same time, urging educators to teach about religion and religious liberty in the context of history, English, government, and other academic disciplines. With the encouragement of the Board of Trustees of the Americans United Research Foundation, using funds provided by concerned organizations and individuals, Dr. Charles Haynes has brought together, in one volume, a wide variety of source materials which will assist the busy classroom instructor who wishes to integrate the story of religious liberty into the curriculum.

The Board of Trustees of the Foundation applauds the nation's teachers and dedicates this guide to them and their students. Through our combined efforts, may we all come to a renewed commitment to the United States Constitution, the Bill of Rights and the life these documents have made possible.

Jimmy R. Allen, President
Robert L. Maddox, Executive Director
Americans United Research Foundation

CONGRESS SHALL
MAKE NO LAW RESPECTING AN
ESTABLISHMENT OF
RELIGION OR PROHIBITING THE
FREE EXERCISE THEREOF . . .

For nearly two hundred years the opening words of the Bill of Rights have charted the course for humanity's boldest and most successful experiment in religious freedom. It has been a long and difficult journey, marred by episodes of religious conflict and oppression, but inspiring in its progress. Today, hundreds of religious groups in the United States flourish in a climate of understanding and liberty unmatched by any nation in history. As we prepare to celebrate the bicentennials of the Constitution in 1987 and the Bill of Rights in 1991, we can take pride in the knowledge that the religious freedom we enjoy is a uniquely American contribution to world civilization.

We must take care, however, not to allow our celebration of past achievement to lull us into a false sense of security. The battle for freedom is never fully won, but must be engaged anew by each generation. In our time we are challenged by a rising tide of religious intolerance, persistent anti-Semitism, and a resurgence of the Ku Klux Klan. A recent incident in Greenwich, Connecticut illustrates the magnitude of the problems we face: a Jew who objected to a large cross on the local firehouse received over seven hundred hate calls and many unsigned letters expressing outrage. "We are a Christian country," wrote one citizen, "and you are our invited guests. Guests don't tell his host how to run his home." Another letter was more blunt: "I'd be a stoker if we would open up an Auschwitz here."[1]

The first line of defense against hate and intolerance is an educated citizenry. Sadly, abundant evidence suggests that many Americans have neither a clear understanding *of* nor a commitment *to* the religion clauses of the First Amendment. A Media General-Associated Press poll taken in 1985 reveals that one in four Americans does not accept the principle of church-state separation. This should come as no surprise when we con-

---

[1]Reported by Nat Hentoff, "Guests in a Christian Country," *The Washington Post,* Jan. 11, 1986.

sider the large numbers of people who are responding to calls for a "Christian America" and supporting efforts to promote sectarian beliefs in the public schools.

Secondary school social studies teachers have a unique opportunity to educate Americans about our heritage of religious freedom. That is why it is disturbing to find religious freedom largely ignored in the social studies curriculum. According to recent studies, a reader of most U.S. history and government texts would gain little insight into the story of religious liberty in America and might well conclude that religion in general has been of little or no consequence in our nation's history.[2]

The neglect of religious freedom in textbooks is ironic given that many contemporary debates about the meaning of the religion clauses revolve around the public schools. If not in social studies, where will young Americans get the historical and constitutional perspectives necessary to form educated opinions about school prayer, equal access, creationism, and similar issues that directly affect their lives?

There are those who express concern about raising these questions in the classroom, believing that the Supreme Court has banned religion from our public schools. These fears are unfounded. What the Court has ruled unconstitutional is the teaching *of* religion in public schools, including such practices as state-mandated prayer and devotional use of the Bible. Objective teaching *about* religion is constitutional and, in fact, encouraged by the Court. In the *Abington School District v. Schempp* decision of 1963, Justice Tom Clark wrote:

> It might well be said that one's education is not complete without a study of comparative religion or the history of religion and its relation to the advancement of civilization. It certainly may be said that the Bible is worthy of study for its literary and historic qualities. Nothing we have said here indicates that such study of the Bible or religion, when presented objectively as part of a secular program of education, may not be effected consistently with the First Amendment.[3]

Silence concerning matters of religion will only breed ignorance and may well endanger one of our most cherished freedoms. To break

---

[2]O. L. Davis, Jr., Gerald Ponder, Lynn M. Burlbaw, Maria Garza-Lubeck, and Alfred Moss, "Looking at History: A Review of Major U.S. History Textbooks" (People for the American Way, 1986). Paul C. Vitz, "Religion and Traditional Values in Public School Textbooks: An Empirical Study" (National Institute of Education Project, 1985). Charles C. Haynes, "Teaching about Religious Freedom" (Americans United Research Foundation, 1985).

[3]For a full discussion of this topic see: Charles R. Kniker, *Teaching About Religion in the Public Schools* (Bloomington, Indiana: Phi Delta Kappa Educational Foundation, 1985).

this silence is not always easy, especially in communities deeply divided by religious freedom questions. These are controversial and complex subjects requiring strong teacher preparation and careful objectivity. Nevertheless, however difficult the task, we must commit ourselves to making the first of what James Madison called the "Great Rights" an integral part of every student's education.

The Americans United Research Foundation offers this book to teachers in time for the bicentennials in the belief that these observances provide a rare opportunity to improve education about freedom of religion. Our sole aim in compiling and distributing this guide is to encourage the inclusion of this vital topic in the social studies curriculum. The background articles and resources included here have been carefully selected for their quality, objectivity and balance. It is our hope that these resources, when used in government and U.S. history courses, will do much to correct the deficiencies of existing textbooks. This is our bicentennial gift to you and to the students of America. Please use it well.

Charles C. Haynes

PART I   BACKGROUND

The story of religious freedom is central to the story of America. Since the days of the first arrivals, immigrants have come to this nation seeking to be free in matters of religious faith and practice. Today we enjoy the fruits of the long struggle waged by many courageous people to secure this fundamental freedom.

What follows are the reflections of two eminent scholars on the meaning of religious freedom in the United States. Robert T. Handy, Professor Emeritus of Church History at Union Theological Seminary, focuses in Chapter 1 on the underlying historical forces that led to the adoption of the religion clauses of the First Amendment. How these clauses have been interpreted by the Supreme Court is discussed in Chapter 2 by Isidore Starr, a lawyer and educator who is widely recognized as the father of law-related education.

1. THE AMERICAN TRADITION OF RELIGIOUS FREEDOM: AN HISTORICAL ANALYSIS

Robert T. Handy

I.

The American tradition of religious freedom was shaped over a long period of time through the interaction of many forces. A major milestone in its history was reached when the First Amendment to the Constitution of the United States went into effect in 1791. The amendment provided that the principle of religious liberty be recognized at the national level, and sought to safeguard the principle through what is generally known as the separation of church and state. Religious freedom thus defined was the result of the working together of diverse causes, and was somewhat differently viewed by various elements in the population. Reflecting on the vast changes in American life since the First Amendment, one can readily see how attitudes toward that amendment could be even more complex now than then. In the century and three-quarters since the crucial congressional debates over that important amendment, not only has the area of the country increased over four times and the population multiplied by nearly fifty, but the religious picture, complex enough then, has become vastly more diversified. The story of the rise of religious liberty and the shaping of the First Amendment has been gone over from many points of view — sometimes with primary emphasis on understanding what happened and sometimes with deliberate intent to find backing for a position already held, but probably more often with a subtle blend of both interests. The present debate about the meaning of religious liberty and the nature of the separation of church and state can be better understood when viewed against the some three and one-half centuries of American experience with reference not only to the important story of the coming of religious freedom but also with attention to later developments in the changing American religious scene.

The majority of the European settlers who came to North American shores in the 17th and 18th centuries did not believe in religious freedom. They accepted as axiomatic the concepts of religious uniformity and of the establishment of the church by the state. The countries which maintained colonies in North America — England, France, and Spain — all had established churches themselves and restricted the freedom of religious minorities. In the English colonies which were to become the United States, the center of concern in this article, the Church of Eng-

11

land was established by law in five (Virginia, Maryland, North Carolina, South Carolina and Georgia), and in part in a sixth (New York). In three of the New England colonies the Congregationalists, a dissenting group in the mother country, established their congregations under the law, not at all breaking with the idea that the one "true" church should be protected and supported by the civil authorities. At times Protestants have been too willing to gloss over this past, and have deserved the sharp rebuke of Perry Miller, "In their original intention, Protestants were intolerant; . . . the Protestant churches did not so much achieve religious liberty as have liberty thrust upon them."[1] While it is not quite accurate to lump all Protestants in this way, for there were minorities who did believe in religious freedom, it is important to realize that for the most part the leaders of English colonization in America believed in religious uniformity and establishment and restricted religious liberty. Against this background the reversal of what had long been considered axiomatic in Western civilization — that established religion was essential to civil order and peace — can be seen for the daring experiment that it was. But what caused this startling and important reversal?

II.

The sources of the tradition of religious liberty and the practice of the separation of church and state in America cannot be neatly analyzed, for they were many and worked in various combinations in differing times and places. In some parts of the land one particular factor may seem to be in evidence while at some other points it scarcely appears, but several others may be seen at work. In some minds, one particular current of thought led to a commitment to religious freedom while in others quite contradictory patterns of thinking led to a similar commitment though the motivation was quite different. Looked at overall, there were at least six major forces or sets of factors at work. Together they wove the fabric of religious freedom and built the much-debated "wall of separation" between church and state in the United States. To neglect any of these is to understand less than the full story of religious liberty; to overemphasize any of them is to pave the way for distorted claims and erroneous impressions.

A.

It is especially difficult to assess the importance of geographical, economic, and political situations on the rise of religious liberty, for they

---

[1] Miller, "The Contribution of the Protestant Churches to Religious Liberty in Colonial," 4 *Church History* 57, 66 (1935).

were ambivalent with respect to church-state matters and often worked or could be exploited for legal establishment. In the history of religious freedom, however, certain pressures stemming primarily from matters of geography, economics, and politics did serve to limit the effectiveness of church establishments and to provide opportunites for the spread of dissent on the one hand and indifference on the other. For example, the vast ocean between the mother country and the dependent Church of England colonial establishments was a serious barrier to good church administration. Inasmuch as no bishops were appointed for the Episcopal Church in America until after the Revolution, this meant that serious lacks in supervision, discipline, and mission and ministerial supply could go for long periods uncorrected. The various expedients used to fill the administrative gap, such as the development of vestries and the use of commissaries, were not highly successful in dealing with the Church's problems. Once across the ocean, however, space again became a problem, this time in the vastness of the new land. As population spread, some parishes grew to immense size, making it difficult for the clergy to deal with the spiritual needs of parishioners in a satisfying way. In New England Congregationalism, on the other hand, church administration was locally controlled, and the ocean served as a barrier against interference from the mother country. But, as in the South, the existence of free space around the colonial settlements tended to work against tight control. Originally towns were laid out compactly with houses grouped centrally and fields outlying, but the extent and availability of land made it preferable for settlers to locate their farms on their own fields where they were not so directly under the watchful eye of pastors and elders.[2]

The desire for economic success also tended to retard efforts to maintain strictly church establishments and keep out dissenters. One of the most famous incidents which illustrates this occurred in New Netherland shortly before it was taken over by the British as New York. The Reformed Church was established in the Dutch colony, and Governor Peter Stuyvesant was determined to keep out sectarian elements, especially Quakers. He seized John Bowne of Flushing; after several months imprisonment Bowne was sent to Holland. But when he appealed to the directors of the West India Company, they disallowed Stuyvesant's repressive measures, and wrote him saying, "We heartily desire that these and other sectaries had remained away, . . . yet we doubt very much whether we can proceed against them vigorously, without

---

[2]Wertenbaker, *The Puritan Oligarchy: The Founding of American Civilization* 43, 184-90 (1947).

diminishing the population and stopping emigration."[3] Without manpower the colony could scarcely succeed economically, so peaceful dissenters had to be tolerated. An even clearer illustration comes from the next century when the Presbyterian leader, Samuel Davies, was persecuted for his religious views in Anglican Virginia. The Lords of Trade in England objected to such treatment, declaring that: "With regard to the affair of Mr. Davies the Presbyterian, as Toleration and a free Exercise of Religion is so valuable a branch of true liberty, and so essential to the enriching and improving of a Trading Nation, it should ever be held sacred in His Majesty's Colonies."[4]

Certain political realities in the colonial period also tended to exert a pressure on the colonies with established churches to exercise a measure of toleration toward dissenters. England was torn by civil and religious strife in the middle of the 17th century, but as W. K. Jordan sums up his massive study on the rise of religious toleration in England, as early as 1660

> the mass of men in England — what might be described as the centre of gravity of opinion — had conceded the case for religious toleration with very few reservations. This intensely revolutionary decision had to be taken, this momentous change in the history of thought had to be accomplished, in point of fact, before the stress and strain so evident in English history for rather more than a century could be ended. The conviction had gained strength in English thought that the ends of national life . . . could not be attained until the divisive and destructive energies of religious conflict had been tamed by toleration.[5]

So developments in the mother country tended to check the zealousness of eager uniformitarians in the colonies. A rather curious and early illustration of this trend was the halting of the execution of Quakers in Boston by King Charles II; with their ultimate weapon thus taken away, the New England Puritan leaders found themselves finally unable to keep the Quakers out. In the next century the English dissenters, who had won a measure of toleration though not yet religious freedom, were watchful lest their gains be taken away or the situation of their fellow believers in America be jeopardized by, for example, the appointment of an Anglican bishop for the colonies. So political factors long frustrated

[3]Letter from the Directors of the West Indian Company to Governor Peter Stuyvesant, April 16, 1663, in Cobb, *The Rise of Religious Liberty in America* 321 (1902).

[4]Letter from William Dawson to the Bishop of London, Aug. 16, 1751, in 1 *Historical Collections Relating to the American Colonial Church* 380 (Perry ed. 1870).

[5]4 Jordan, *The Development of Religious Toleration in England* 467 (1940).

the various campaigns to get "episcopoi" for the Episcopal Church.[6] In such rather negative ways, certain geographical, economic, and political forces operated in the direction of religious liberty, chiefly by inhibiting the effectiveness of established churches, increasing the area of toleration, and thereby allowing greater religious pluralism in the colonies.

B.

The sheer fact of religious pluralism was itself a major, perhaps the major, single force which opened the door to religious liberty. That there was no one religious body with a hold on the majority of the population when the republic was founded has a lot to do with insuring that no national establishment of religion could be attempted. The late Perry Miller put the matter with his customary provocativeness when, in dealing with freedom in both the educational and the religious spheres, he said:

> The point is, to put it baldly, that both in education and in religion, we didn't aspire to freedom, we didn't march steadily toward it, we didn't unfold the inevitable propulsion of our hidden nature: we stumbled into it. We got a variety of sects as we got a college catalogue: the denominations and the sciences multiplied until there was nothing anybody could do about them. Wherefore we gave them permission to exist, and called the result freedom of the mind. Then we found, to our vast delight, that by thus negatively surrendering we could congratulate ourselves on a positive and heroic victory. So we stuck the feather in our cap and called it Yankee Doodle.[7]

Generally in sections where there were established churches, especially in the New England Puritan colonies and in Anglican Virginia and Maryland, religious pluralism was less in evidence than in the middle colonies and Rhode Island. As early as 1741, when Pennsylvania was just threescore years old, the Moravian leader Count Ludwig von Zinzendorf was startled at the religious pluralism he found in that colony. He wrote, "All shades of Sectarians exist here down to open infidelity."[8]

---

[6]The story of the campaigns for an American Episcopal bishop is well told by Bridenbaugh, *Mitre and Septre: Transatlantic Faiths, Ideas, Personalities, and Politics 1689-1775* (1962).

[7]Miller, Calhoun, Pusey & Niebuhr, *Religion and Freedom of Thought* 15-16 (1954).

[8]The quotation is from Count von Zinzendorf's list of different sects present in Pennsylvania during his visit in the years 1741-1742. Quoted in 1 Sachse, *The German Sectarians of Pennsylvania 1708-1742*, 442 (1899).

"Besides the English, Swedish and German Lutherans, and the Scotch, Dutch and German Reformed, there were Armenians, Baptists, 'Vereinigte Vlaaminger en Waterlander', Mennonites from Danzig, Arians, Socinians, Schwenckfelders, German Old Tunkers, New Tunkers, New Lights, Inspired, Sabbatarians or Seventh-Day Baptists, Hermits, Independents, and Free Thinkers."[9] That gives a picture of the religious diversities if one looks at the various ethnic forms of one denominational family and gathers up all the sectarian movements in what was probably the most pluralistic colony. A clearer over-all view of the nature of American religious multiplicity at the close of the colonial period can be glimpsed by studying the estimates of the number of congregations of each denominational persuasion at that time. There were more than seven hundred Congregational churches, located chiefly in New England. There were between four and five hundred each of Presbyterian, Baptist, and Anglican churches. Lutheran, German Reformed, and Quaker congregations numbered between two hundred and two hundred and fifty each. Dutch Reformed numbered about one hundred and twenty-five congregations, Moravians just over eighty, Mennonites just under seventy, and Roman Catholics nearly sixty. Then there were a number of scattered small groups with at most a handful of congregations; Methodist societies, for example, were just breaking free from nominal ties with the Church of England to achieve independent status in America in 1784. These estimates are only approximations, but they do serve to indicate that the religious pluralism of the country was overwhelmingly a Protestant one. Roman Catholics numbered about one per cent of the population and were just emerging from a period in which they had suffered legal disabilities. There had been Jewish settlers in the colonies very early, but they were still a tiny minority at the close of the colonial period—perhaps one-twentieth of one per cent of the population.[10] Sometimes when looking back at the last quarter of the 18th century, we read back the quite different religious pluralism of a later time into that setting; the pluralism then was prevailingly within the Protestant tradition. But it was great enough to make it impossible for any one group seriously to seek to establish itself as a national religion. Furthermore, the growing religious pluralism made untenable the continuation for very long of those state establishments of religion which survived the 18th century.

[9]1 Sachse, *op. cit, supra* note 8, at 442.

[10]The estimates are made on the basis of Gaustad, *Historical Atlas of Religion in America* 1-36, 158-61, app. B (1962). Also see Sperry, *Religion in America* app. B (1946).

C.

So far, two sets of forces which contributed in a practical and somewhat negative way to religious freedom have been analyzed, but there were Americans of various religious perspectives who were positive believers in religious freedom and who acted forthrightly for it. Because at times their contributions have been over-assessed, there is no warrant for going to the other extreme and minimizing what they did. For certain Protestant voices, particularly those from the left wing of the Reformation (Mennonites) and from the left wing of Puritanism (at first chiefly Baptists and Quakers, later others of Puritan Calvinist background), were from the early decades of colonial history lifted in favor of religious freedom. The 16th-century Anabaptists in Europe broke with the church-state system, often suffering intense persecution as a result; their descendants in America, the Mennonites, continued to witness and to work for religious freedom.[11] Because much of Protestant America was Calvinist in theological orientation, the biblical and theological arguments for religious freedom as developed by Baptists and Quakers were especially significant and helped to win others of generally Calvinist orientation from acceptance of prevailing views of establishment to religious freedom. The leadership of such representatives of left-wing Puritanism as Roger Williams, John Clarke, and William Penn in the struggle for liberty has long been recognized and need not be stressed here.[12] Winthrop S. Hudson has demonstrated how men of this stamp in England and America developed ideas of religious freedom and the separation of church and state from theological premises generally accepted by most Protestants, particularly those of Calvinist stamp, including Presbyterians and Reformed.[13] Such men came to the belief that their grasp of religious truth was imperfect and fallible; they expected to discover yet more truth in the Word of God and thus felt the need to be free to change. Believing firmly with all Calvinists in the sovereignty of God and the sinfulness of man, they concluded that the church should be dependent upon God alone and hence independent of the state. They also affirmed that the church should be voluntary in membership, made up of the convinced only. At first these radicals were sharply resisted, but then their arguments began to win others to their views. They played some

---

[11]A good discussion of the Mennonite posture on church and state is found in T. Sanders, *Protestant Concepts of Church and State* 75-112 (1964).

[12]See, e.g., 1 Stokes, *Church and State in the United States* 194-208 (1950).

[13]Hudson, *The Great Tradition of the American Churches* 42-62 (1953); see also Hudson, "John Locke — Preparing the Way for the Revolution," 42 *Journal of Presbyterian History* 19, 24-28 (1964).

part in the devotion to freedom that many American Presbyterians showed by the later 18th century. Probably the majority of Presbyterians in the colonial period were of Scotch-Irish descent. In Scotland the Presbyterian Church was (and is) established, but during the time in which many Scots resided in Ireland before migrating again, they were forced to support an Anglican establishment there that claimed the allegiance of only a small part of the population. Many of them came to heartily dislike church establishment and were ready to support a policy of separation. Other American Presbyterians were of English Puritan background; a combination of theological and practical considerations led numbers of them, like the eloquent Samuel Davies, to participate in the struggle for religious freedom.[14]

Christians of other than Calvinist orientation, however, could also appreciate that on the American scene freedom of religion was highly desirable. Maryland, where later (1702) the Church of England was established, was of course founded under Roman Catholic auspices as a haven for Catholics, though Protestants numerically were the larger group in the colony from the beginnings of settlement in 1634. Hence the goodwill of Protestants was necessary for the success of the venture. The proprietors, the first two Lords Baltimore, George Calvert and his son Cecilius, were men of liberal spirit and advocated a policy of toleration for their colony. The growing strength of Puritan elements in the colony, threatening this policy, led to some forthright statements concerning toleration, especially the Maryland Toleration Act of 1649.[15] A Catholic historian has given a fair assessment of the nature of the Catholic stance in Maryland in these words: "Catholics did not conceive of tolerance with the complete theoretical dedication of a Roger Williams in Rhode Island. Yet when they asserted the legal respecting of the individual conscience for the sake of serving the common good, there would seem to have been philosophical commitment as well as political expediency involved."[16] American Catholics in the colonial and revolutionary periods continued to press for religious freedom. The first American Roman Catholic bishop, John Carroll, sincerely believed that religious freedom was best for the nation; on a number of occasions he spoke of his "earnest regard to preserve inviolate forever, in our new empire, the great principle of religious freedom."[17] He firmly believed that the

---

[14]On the nature of colonial Presbyterianism see Trinterud, *The Forming of an American Tradition* (1949). On Samuel Davies see 1 Stokes, *op. cit. supra* note 12, at 208-16.

[15]1 *The Archives of Maryland* 244 (Browne ed. 1883).

[16]Browne, "Catholicism in the United States," in *Religion in American Life* 74-75 (Smith & Jamison eds. 1961).

[17]Letter from Pacificus to Mr. Fenno (Publisher), June 10, 1789, in Gazette of the United States, June 10, 1789, p. 65, col. 3; 1 Guilday, *The Life and Times of John Carroll* 368 (1922).

United States must place the preservation of her liberties and her government "on the attachment of mankind to their political happiness, to the security of their persons and their property which is 'independent of any religious doctrines and not restrained by any.' "[18] All of these instances illustrate how churches which in Europe continued to support establishment patterns could in North America advocate religious liberty.

D.

Another group of forceful advocates of religious liberty came from a quite different frame of reference than those who were motivated primarily by Christian principles. The importance of Enlightenment thought in the American Revolutionary and Constitutional periods has long been emphasized, and that those strongly influenced by Enlightenment philosophy were often leading spokesmen for religious freedom and for church-state separation has long been stressed. In a recent comment on the rise of the Enlightenment and its challenge to revealed religion, historian Crane Brinton declared, "the basic structure of Christian belief survived, however, not without heresies and schisms, until, roughly, the late seventeenth century when there arose in our society what seems to me clearly to be a new religion, certainly related to, descended from, and by many reconciled with, Christianity. I call this religion simply Enlightenment, with a capital E."[19] For a variety of reasons, many who became essentially imbued with the perspectives of the new religion, including many whom we number among the Founding Fathers of our country, remained at least nominally related to their traditional church homes while they operated largely from the perspectives of the new. Thomas Jefferson, who remained in loose connection with Anglicanism while adopting an essentially Unitarian theological position, penned the famous Virginia Bill for Establishing Religious Freedom, which was passed in 1785.[20] It stated in part:

That no man shall be compelled to frequent or support any religious worship, place, or ministry whatsoever, nor shall be enforced, restrained, molested, or burthened in his body or goods, nor shall otherwise suffer on account of his religious opinions or belief; but that all men shall be free to profess, and by argument to maintain, their opinions in matters of religion,

[18]Melville, *John Carroll of Baltimore* 89 (1955).

[19]Brinton, "Many Mansions," 69 *Am. Hist. Rev.* 309, 315 (1964).

[20]12 Laws of Va. ch. 34, at 84 (Hening 1823).

and that the same shall in no wise diminish, enlarge, or effect their civil capacities.[21]

The bill reflects the thought of the Enlightenment, but was written to secure wide support among believers in religious freedom of whatever orientation. Indeed, as William Warren Sweet once concluded, "It was the leadership of such Lockian disciples as Jefferson and Madison, backed by an overwhelming left-wing Protestant public opinion, that was responsible for writing the clauses guaranteeing religious freedom into the new state constitutions and finally into the fundamental law of the land."[22] That summary may be a little too neat for I am arguing here that there are other matters also to take into account, but it does point to an important element in the whole story.

The spread of Enlightenment thought was at least one of the reasons for the decline of revealed religion in the 18th century. Many historians of religion have explained how weak the influence of organized religion became during the Revolutionary period in America. It has been estimated that probably less than ten per cent of the population were active members of any church in the last quarter of the 18th century.[23] One must be careful not to read 20th-century realities back into an 18th-century situation — church membership generally meant considerably more then than now, and the active constituency of a congregation often outnumbered its formal membership. Also, problems arising from both frontier and war situations must be taken into account in assessing the low ebb of church life at the time. Yet even making allowances, still one must conclude that the decline of revealed religion and the rise of deism reflect the popularity of Enlightenment thought at the time. It was in an atmosphere in which Enlightenment influence was strong that the struggle for religious liberty was largely won and the patterns of church-state separation worked out.

E.

Any effort to single out the forces that worked together to bring about religious freedom in the nation runs the risk of oversimplification unless it is stressed that these forces often interacted on one another. This can be especially seen in the histories of those four English colonies which did not have established churches: Rhode Island, Pennsylvania, New Jersey, and Delaware. In these, the thought and action of those

---

[21] 12 Laws of Va. ch. 34, 2m at 86 (Hening 1823).

[22] Sweet, "The Protestant Churches," 256 *Annals* 45 (1948).

[23] Littell, *From State Churches to Pluralism* 29-33 (1962).

committed to religious liberty as a matter of principle combined with the facts of religious pluralism to provide working examples of successful societies without established churches. What had long seemed axiomatic in Western civilization was shown not necessarily to be true. It was demonstrated that one could have civil peace and order without state churches. Figures of the Enlightenment made a lot of these examples; Franklin and Jefferson, for instance, called attention to them. But thoughtful members of churches which normally sought establishment could also get the point. One Colonel Morris, a prominent Anglican layman, for example, after observing the quarrels stirred up over the stipend for religion provided by the colony of New York, wrote that he believed that his church would have "at this day been in much better condition had there been no Act in her favor; for in the Jersies and Pennsylvania where there is no Act in her favor, there is four times the number of Churchmen than there is in this province of New York, and they are so most of them upon principle."[24] The patterns of freedom and separation were not only proved to work in those four colonies, but some came to believe that such patterns worked better for the churches than did the ways of establishment. The models provided by the four colonies were created through the operation of various of the forces here being analyzed, but, once created, they served further to stimulate and strengthen those forces.

F.

The Great Awakening, that remarkable movement of religious revival which swept through the colonies in a series of waves which touched every section of the country at one time or another in the half century just preceding the Revolution, tended on the whole to work in the direction of greater religious freedom. Awakeners put stress on a warmhearted, practical religion and did much to stimulate a generally pietistic understanding of Christianity in denominations of quite diverse historical backgrounds. The intercolonial character of the awakenings served incidentally to lower barriers between the separate colonies and was one of the forces preparing the way for larger national unity. Leading Awakeners, men like Theodore Frelinghuysen, Jonathan Edwards, the Tennents, George Whitefield, and Samuel Davies, worked together across denominational and sectional lines. The Great Awakening was of course primarily a movement of religious renewal, but in a general way it played a part in the struggle for religious freedom. Alice M. Baldwin has summarized the matter in these words:

[24]Letter from Colonel Morris to the Secretary of the Society for Propagating the Gospel, Feb. 20, 1711, in 3 *Ecclesiastical Records of the State of New York 1910* (Hastings ed. 1902).

The Great Awakening with its consequent confusions, political strife, and doctrinal discussions had stimulated men to new and lively thinking in religious and civil affairs. It had brought with it much intolerance, yet out of it had grown a passionate conviction in man's right to freedom of conscience and a struggle, partly successful, to obtain it.[25]

There were both theoretical and practical aspects in the contribution of the Awakening to freedom. Theologically, Awakeners stressed a radical doctrine of human sin, which by underlining the insight that no man is good enough to govern others without the careful definition and limitation of his powers disposed many Christians to look with favor on the freedom movements of their day. Practically, the awakenings led to the increase in the number and size of many nonestablished churches so that the claims of those that remained established became more and more difficult to maintain. After study of the Awakening in Virginia, Wesley M. Gewehr concluded that: "The Great Awakening gave rise to popular forms of church government and thus accustomed people to self-government in their religious habits. The alliance of Church and State, the identification of religious with civil institutions, was found to be detrimental to the cause of religion."[26]

III.

The many forces making for religious freedom and for separation of church and state combined in various ways at the state level. As has been noted, in four of the English colonies there were no formal establishments from the beginning. During the Revolutionary period, vigorous drives to remove the state establishments which remained were undertaken. A hotly contested struggle for disestablishment was carried on in Virginia. This was an especially significant move because the Anglican establishment had long been in effect and because the leadership of Jefferson and Madison was active in the drive. An important turning point in the struggle was the adoption of the Virginia Bill of Rights[27] in 1776. The disestablishment process began the same year. But there was considerable support for a plan for general financial assistance to religion on the part of the state without discrimination. Patrick Henry was the eloquent leader of that group, but Jefferson and Madison were to prevail.

---

[25]Baldwin, *The New England Clergy and the American Revolution* 80 (1928).

[26]Gewehr, *The Great Awakening in Virginia* 187 (1930).

[27]2 *Charters and Constitutions of the United States* 1908 (Poore ed. 1878).

Jefferson drafted the Bill for Establishing Religious Freedom while Madison was conspicuous in securing its adoption late in 1785 by a three to one margin. Though the work of the liberal leaders was of course important, the great number of petitions and memorials to the legislature on behalf of the bill from many Baptists, Presbyterians, and Quakers was influential in the final result, and the agreement of many Episcopalians to the bill was evident in the clear majority by which it was passed. All of the other Church of England establishments (except Maryland, where the Episcopal Church enjoyed a favored status until the early 19th century) were terminated by the time of the ratification of the First Amendment, but the deep-rooted Congregational establishments of New England survived longest of all. The New Hampshire church establishment was dropped in 1816. In Connecticut, Congregationalism and federalism were allied in the effort to maintain the Standing Order of clergy. The growing strength of Baptists, Methodists, and Episcopalians finally showed itself in a political overturn of 1817, and the next year brought a new constitution which provided for the separation of church and state. The Massachusetts struggle was a long-drawn-out affair, and not until 1833 was a constitutional amendment separating church from state finally ratified. In most of these states, before final disestablishment other church bodies beside the major one were granted or offered some subsidy from public funds in what has been called multiple establishment, but at the time such measures were all finally rejected in favor of full separation.

IV.

On the national level, however, the forces making for religious freedom and separation were dominant from the beginning of our independent life. At the Constitutional Convention in 1787 there was apparently not much discussion concerning religion. Article VI of the Constitution carries the statement that "no religious Test shall ever be required as a Qualification to any Office or public Trust under the United States."[28] But during the preparation and passage of the first ten amendments religious matters came under more intense discussion. A vast literature has gathered around the origin and meaning of the religion clauses of the First Amendment.[29] Madison would probably have liked the amendment to be extended to exclude state church establish-

[28] U.S. Constitution, art VI, 3.

[29] A glimpse of this vast literature can be found in the footnotes and bibliographies of such recent books (of varying points of view) as Katz, *Religion and American Constitutions* (1964); Kurland, *Religion and the Law* (1962); Marnell, *The First Amendment* (1964); and *The Supreme Court on Church & State* (Tussman ed. 1962).

23

ments, but the Senate was unwilling to allow this. It is interesting to observe that while the Senate was discussing the religion clauses, a number of efforts were made to have them read in such a way that, while there would be no one national religious establishment, more than one church might be aided or established. All such efforts were defeated. The form in which the religion clauses first came to the Senate from the House of Representatives was as follows: "Congress shall make no law establishing religion, or prohibiting the free exercise thereof, nor shall the rights of conscience be infringed."[30] When the Senate took up the matter on September 3, 1789, a move to substitute the words "One Religious Sect or Society in preference to others" for "religion" was rejected.[31] Then other efforts were made to change the proposal. One read, "Congress shall make no law establishing any particular denomination of religion in preference to another, or prohibiting the free exercise thereof, nor shall the rights of conscience be infringed."[32] This was defeated, but at this point the third clause was dropped, for apparently some feared it might upset the remaining state establishments. On September 9, the Senate passed this wording: "Congress shall make no law establishing articles of faith or a mode of worship, or prohibiting the free exercise of religion."[33] The House of Representatives would not accept this, and a joint committee worked out the final form of the religion clauses as they were to be incorporated into the First Amendment and ratified in 1791: "Congress shall make no law respecting an establishment of religion, or prohibiting the free exercise thereof."[34] Not only had any provision for a nationally established religion been rejected, but efforts to make possible public support of all equally had been specifically defeated.

V.

There is a tendency in current debates about church and state to move directly from 1791 to the present without much consideration of the intervening history and thus to assume that the general religious situation now is somehow basically what it was then. This leads to the obscuring of certain fundamental developments in American life which very much influence present attitudes and opinions on the issues of religious freedom and on the way we read the First Amendment. Two

---

[30]S. Jour. 1st Sess. 116 (1789).

[31]Ibid

[32]Id. at 117.

[33]Id. at 129.

[34]Id. at 145. The story has been told in detail by Butts, *The American Tradition in Religion and Education* 78-91 (1950).

things in particular will here be emphasized: the way many church leaders in the 19th century continued to assume that America was really a Protestant nation and pressed for making it more fully so, and then the shift from what I have called a Protestant pluralism in religion to a radical pluralism[35] in which other forms of institutional religion have come to occupy major places in American religious life.

Protestants in general accepted disestablishment with varying degrees of enthusiasm. But nevertheless they tended to cling to one of the basic assumptions on which establishment had been based. As Sidney E. Mead has convincingly shown:

> Establishment rested upon two basic assumptions: that the existence and well-being of any society depends upon a body of commonly shared religious beliefs — the nature of man, his place in the cosmos, his destiny, and his conduct toward his fellow men — and that the only guarantee that these necessary beliefs will be sufficiently inculcated is to put the coercive power of the state behind the institution responsible for their definition, articulation and inculcation.[36]

Disestablishment meant the giving up of the second of these assumptions, that concerning coercion, but it did not necessarily mean giving up the first, as to the necessity for commonly shared basic religious ideas. Many Protestant leaders understood America to be in tradition and spirit a Protestant nation, and in the early 19th century they set themselves to task of making America Christian with great energy and determination. They had given up the method of coercion for the method of persuasion — they accepted the voluntary method in religion. As Mead has aptly put it, "Voluntaryism is the necessary corollary of religious freedom."[37] What could not be done by law, they asserted, could be done by voluntary effort. Reacting against the spirit and philosophy of the Enlightenment as leading to French infidelity and the terror of the French Revolution, they mounted in the "Second Great Awakening" a counteroffensive against all enemies of "true" Christianity — among whom they often numbered Roman Catholics. Utilizing the techniques of revivalism, they saw with satisfaction a steady rise in the percentage of church members in the population. Drawing upon the British example of using voluntary societies as a way of getting things done, they organized a vast network of voluntary societies to promote various, interre-

[35]See text, p. 250 supra.

[36]Mead, *The Lively Experiment* 63 (1963).

[37]Id. at 113.

lated Protestant causes of all kinds. They were pleased to find Christian influence strengthening in the moral patterns of the nation, for the societies were not only concerned with Bible reading, missions, and Sunday schools but also with moral and social reform.[38] Clinging firmly to the principle of religious liberty, they nevertheless believed that by the pressure of public opinion they could Christianize the nation along the lines of central Protestant beliefs and attitudes which, with some variations, were the common property of the denominations. In the period from about 1830 to the Civil War, or approximately in the middle third of the 19th century, their efforts were crowned with considerable success. Their influence was widely felt in the cultural, political, and educational life of the nation. As Wilson Smith has recently put it, "At few times in our history has the distinction between the religious and the secular been as clouded as in the three decades before the Civil War. Public men brought sectarian judgments and theological compulsions to bear upon their decisions."[39]

These developments have recently been examined with considerable care by several historians. In a particularly important article which deals chiefly with New England in this period and is entitled "'The True American Union' of Church and State: The Reconstruction of the Theocratic Tradition," James F. Maclear has advanced the thesis that in the early years of the 19th century Congregational churchmen

> sought to eclipse demands for "religious liberty" (already largely conceded in their view) with appeals for the preservation of a Christian civilization. Indeed, so numerous, able, and vocal were conservative spokesmen that though church and state were finally separated, little surrender of Puritan axioms was necessary. Thus the older New England tradition, now adjusted and modernized, flourished and spread, surrounding legal separation with the ancient Puritan assumptions, all proclaiming the United States a broadly confessional republic, with "Moses and Aaron united in counsel . . . the true American union, of which no Christian and no patriot can ever be ashamed."[40]

Maclear supports his argument with a series of quotations from leaders

---

[38]On the voluntary societies, organized into a "benevolent empire" with interlocking directorates, see Barnes, *The Antislavery Impulse* (1933); Cole, *The Social Ideas of the Northern Evangelists* (1954); and Cross, *The Burned-Over District* (1950).

[39]W. Smith, *Professors & Public Ethics* 3 (1956).

[40]28 *Church History* 41 (1959). The quotation within the quotation is from Humphrey, *Miscellaneous Discourses and Reviews* 128-29 (1834).

in American religious and political life at that time. Bela Bates Edwards, for example, could declare in 1848:

> Perfect religious liberty does not imply that the government of the country is not a Christian government. The Christian Sabbath is here recognized by the civil authorities. . . . Most if not all of our constitutions . . . proceed on the basis of the truth of the Christian religion. Christianity has been affirmed to be part and parcel of the law of the land. . . . There is convincing evidence to show that this real, though indirect, connection between the State and Christianity is every year acquiring additional strength, is attended with less and less exception and remonstrance.[41]

And Daniel Webster, while unsuccessfully contesting the right of a Philadelphia philanthropist to establish a secular orphanage, could exclaim, "Christianity, general, tolerant Christianity, Christianity independent of sects and parties, that Christianity to which the sword and the fagot are unknown, general tolerant Christianity, is the law of the land."[42] Though the "true American union" perhaps found its most vigorous advocates in New England, in other parts of the land there were many voices uttering the same point of view and many hands at work for the same goals.[43] A close alliance of religion and culture was worked out, and Protestantism took on many of the aspects of a culture-religion.

The American public school system, designed to provide free, tax-supported basic education for all was largely founded and energetically extended in that period. Traditionally, of course, education was the child of the church, but in the 19th century Protestants with but few exceptions accepted and became staunch supporters of public education. Looking back, some contemporary observers have interpreted this as a great surrender of education by the church to the state. Francis X. Curran, for example, speaks of "a revolutionary development in the history of education and in the history of Christianity: the surrender by American Protestantism during the past century of the control of popular elementary education to the state."[44] But such interpretations, if lifted

---

[41] *Writings of Professor B.B. Edwards* 49 (Park ed. 1853).

[42] Argument of Daniel Webster before the Supreme Court of the United States in *Vidal v. Girard's Ex'rs*, 43 U.S. (2 How.) 61, Feb. 13, 1844, in *Webster's Great Speeches* 530 (Whipple ed. 1879).

[43] See, e.g., Bodo, *The Protestant Clergy and Public Issues* (1954); Hertzberg, Marty & Moody, *The Outbursts That Await Us* 33-44 (1963).

[44] Curran, *Preface to* Curran, *The Churches and the Schools: American Protestantism and Popular Elementary Education* at V (1954).

out of historical context, may easily fail to take account of the centrality of Protestantism in the culture of the time. Protestant supporters for the most part did not understand the development of the public school with their encouragement as a relinquishing of a task they should do, however later generations may view it. They felt that the essentially Protestant culture could be depended on and that a generally Christian tone, especially with respect to morality, would certainly be maintained in public schools. Education was one of the major concerns of the leaders of the voluntary societies, and it was believed that the improvement of education at all levels, including that of elementary public education, would contribute to the cause of Christianization. Many home missions leaders, for example, took time off from their religious tasks to play important roles in the shaping of public school systems in Western States, returning to their missionary posts when the work was well started.[45]

Thus the patterns of Protestant pluralism were maintained and extended. In many ways, the middle third of the 19th century was more of an "American Protestant age" than was the colonial period with its established churches — though of course it was not such in a legal sense. Already, to be sure, the basis of the Protestant dominance was being radically undermined as increasingly larger numbers of non-Protestants were streaming into the country. Certain of the anti-Catholic riots show a basic Protestant anxiety as the *status quo* seemed threatened by the invasion of aliens. Catholicism was already the largest single American denomination by 1850, but not until the 20th century was the minority mentality to be escaped.

VI.

In the last hundred years, however, the patterns of religious pluralism have decisively shifted from one in which the Protestant churches were the dominant units to one of radically different character. The vast floods of immigration in the latter part of the 19th century and in the early years of the 20th century brought large numbers of Roman Catholics, Jews, Eastern Orthodox, and religiously unaffiliated persons into the country. In the first fifteen years of the present century, the immigration intake for a year surpassed the one million mark no less than six times.[46]

Also, largely since the Civil War, the impact of scientific, evolutionary naturalistic, and critical historical thinking disrupted the predominance of traditional Protestant patterns of thought. Some Protestant

---

[45]Goodykoontz, *Home Missions on the American Frontier* 361-405 (1939).

[46]See 1916 *Commissioner Gen. of Immigration Ann. Rep.* 76-77.

leaders rejected the new trends and sought to maintain the old ways by determined use of the patterns of revivalism. But others sought to come to terms with the new currents of thought and life. They spear-headed the rise of liberalism, which in many respects was an attempt to relate inherited Protestant theology to the intellectual life of the time so that modern men could continue to find a place in the church. The Protestant social gospel, which reached its peak in the early decades of this century under the leadership of Washington Gladden and Walter Rauschenbusch, was not only an attempt to deal with the social problems of industrial America in a creative way from Christian premises, but it was also an effort to present in a relevant way the dream of a Christian America.

Conservatives and liberals could join in a somewhat uneasy alliance in the effort to make America still more Christian. They supported lively movements which were reminiscent of the 19th century voluntary societies, though often more closely and in some cases, as the Federal Council of Churches (founded 1908), officially related to the churches. Gaius Glenn Atkins, remembering the glow of those years of continuing Protestant confidence, once said:

> The first fifteen years of the twentieth century may sometime be remembered in America as the Age of Crusades. There were a superabundance of zeal, a sufficiency of good causes, unusual moral idealism, excessive confidence in mass movements and leaders with rare gifts of popular appeal. . . . The air was full of banners, and the trumpets called from every camp. . . . Twentieth century church crusades were also a continuation, in social, moral and even political regions, of nineteenth century evangelism.[47]

A strong belief in the coming of the kingdom of God filled many Protestant hearts — conservatives held it in traditional eschatological terms while liberals tended to interpret the kingdom as a more perfect social order within history. In this wave of crusading confidence the real meaning of basic changes in American life and thought was largely obscured. The hope of continuing the synthesis of Protestantism with American culture was high. When America entered the First World War, the churches threw themselves into it as the greatest crusade of all, one for the preservation of democracy and Christianity.

After the war was over, however, recognition that patterns of thought indifferent or hostile to Protestantism had won many followers

---

[47]Atkins, *Religion in Our Times* 156-157 (1932).

in America and upset or alienated many of Protestant background could not long be delayed. Nor could the meaning of the new strength of Roman Catholicism, which had fully proven its Americanism in the excitement of the war and found new unity, long be evaded. Protestant confidence sagged sharply in the face of these developments of the 1920's; as one Protestant historian has vividly described what happened:

> Nothing is more striking than the astonishing reversal in the position occupied by the churches and the role played by religion in American life which took place before the new century was well under way. By the nineteen twenties, the contagious enthusiasm which had been poured into the Student Volunteer Movement, the Layman's Missionary Movement, the Interchurch World Movement, and other organized activities of the churches had largely evaporated.[48]

During that period of slump, which I have elsewhere called the religious depression,[49] church leaders at last had to recognize that Protestantism was no longer in any sense the national religion — though André Siegfried could call it that as late as 1927.[50] Will Herberg has summarized the meaning of the transition that has taken place in these words: "In net effect, Protestantism today no longer regards itself either as a religious movement sweeping the continent or as a national church representing the religious life of the people; Protestantism understands itself today primarily as one of the three religious communities in which twentieth century America has come to be divided."[51] It is, of course, oversimplification to refer only to the three religious communities — to be fully accurate one would have to add Orthodoxy; delineate the differences between Negro and white Protestantism; note the distinctions between such movements as Unitarianism, Jehovah's Witnesses, Mormonism, and Christian Science and the traditional Protestant denominations; and pay some attention to the growing strength of minority movements outside the Judaeo-Christian tradition entirely. The point in the present connection is clear enough: the fundamentally Protestant religious pluralism of 1791 and of the first part of the 19th century had yielded to a radical pluralism by the middle of the 20th century.

Tensions in matters of church and state often arise today when

---

[48]Hudson, *The Great Tradition of the American Churches* 196 (1953).

[49]Handy, "The American Religion Depression, 1925-1935," 29 *Church History* 3-16 (1960).

[50]Siegfried, *American Comes of Age* 33 (1927).

[51]Herberg, *Protestant — Catholic — Jew* 139-40 (1955).

practices rooted in the American Protestant age of the 19th century persist into the present. This was forcefully stated in a recent report adopted by the General Assembly of the United Presbyterian Church in the United States of America:

> Some problems existing in colonial times have been solved or have disappeared: for example, the legal establishment of a state church. But a number of specific contemporary problems of church and state are the product of the early Protestant era of American history. Sunday laws, for example, were the creation of Puritan culture. Although held by the Supreme Court to be a safeguard for labor, historical responsibility for Sunday laws lies with the Puritans and their descendants. Tax exemption for church property, clerical exemption from military service, censorship, the use of public property for religious displays, the evaluation of the fitness of candidates for public office on the basis of religious affiliation, and a host of other pressing questions are the heritage of Protestant predominance in the earlier era of American history. While the birth control dispute has been thrown into the foreground in a new way by the moral position adopted by the Roman Catholic bishops, it is necessary to acknowledge that most of the laws that raise the church-state issues in our time are not the product of the massive Catholic immigration but of an earlier era to which our own [Presbyterian] tradition is akin. Even without the formidable new Roman Catholic opinion group, the advancing secular spirit of American democracy would have demanded that the heirs of the Puritans rethink old positions.[52]

Quite naturally, Catholics, Jews, militant secularists and other minorities (that is, from the perspective of main-line Protestantism) have protested the survival of specifically Protestant practices in public life and in the public schools. Hence have arisen a number of highly publicized and highly significant Supreme Court decisions of which perhaps the best known are *Everson v. Board of Education*,[53] the school bus case; *Illinois ex rel. McCollum v. Board of Education*[54] and *Zorach v. Clauson*,[55] con-

---

[52]Special Committee on Church and State, "Report of the Special Committee on Relations Between Church and State in the U.S.A.," in 1 *The United Presbyterian Church in the United States of America, General Assembly, Journal 1963*, 180, 203-04.

[53]333 U.S. 1 (1948).

[54]333 U.S. 203 (1948).

[55]343 U.S. 306 (1952).

cerning released-time programs of religious instruction; *Engel v. Vitale*,[56] concerning the New York Regents prayer; and the companion cases of *School Dist. v. Schempp*[57] and *Murray v. Curlett*,[58] concerning Bible reading and prayer in public school. Some discussions of what the Supreme Court has done interpreting the First Amendment seem to ignore the historical situation at the time of its passage or the radically changed historical situation since. Recognition of these sweeping changes, so briefly alluded to here, has been slow in coming to many Americans, perhaps especially to Protestants in certain areas of the country where older rural patterns have persisted longer and in certain churches of conservative orientation. But the earlier period of Protestant pluralism in which fusions of Protestantism with culture could pass unchallenged is over, and fruitful discussions of the proper way to relate church and state in America today must take account of the historical realities which helped to shape the First Amendment and which continue to influence the way it has been and is being interpreted today.

[56]370 U.S. 421 (1963).
[57]374 U.S. 203 (1963).
[58]Ibid.

2. TEETERING ON THE WALL OF SEPARATION

by Isidore Starr

T he proper relation of church and state has been a persistent dilemma for our nation, and especially for the Supreme Court. Justices have often seemed to diverge sharply in trying to balance the claims of religion and law. For example, Justice Wiley Rutledge, who served on the Court in the 1940s, wrote " . . . we have staked the very existence of our country on the faith that complete separation between the state and religion is best for the state and best for religion."

His colleague on the High Court, William O. Douglas, took a different tack: "We are a religious people whose institutions presuppose a Supreme Being. . . . When the state encourages religious instruction or cooperates with religious authorities . . . it follows the best of our traditions."

One Justice reminds us of the metaphoric wall of separation and the need to remember the theocratic excesses of the past; the other reminds us of our religious heritage and the need to respect our religious roots.

We may wonder whether these standpoints are complementary or irreconcilable, but one thing is sure: this kind of complex, multifaceted response to church/state dilemmas has been characteristic of the Court over the years. In trying to preserve both the free exercise of religion and its disestablishment, and in trying to protect the rights of believers and doubters alike, the Court has been confronted with issues ranging from parochiaid to polygamy, from school prayers to conscientious objectors.

The Constitutional Debate

Naturally, the Constitution provides a major source of guidance to the Court as it wrestles with these dilemmas. Those who wrote the Constitution and the Bill of Rights were well aware of the church-state conundrum, and tried to resolve it with three sweeping statements.

The first is the concluding sentence in Article VI: " . . . but no religious Test shall ever be required as a Qualification to an Office or public Trust under the United States." This is the only substantive reference to religion in the body of the Constitution. The only other reference is to "the year of our Lord" in Article VII, but that is merely customary usage rather than a substantive provision. Contrary to popular opinion, the Presidential Oath in the Constitution contains no mention of "So help me God." Initiated by George Washington, it has simply become the custom to add this phrase in the swearing-in ceremony.

The other two religion clauses are found in the First Amendment.

They are better known than Article VI and more widely applicable: "Congress shall make no law respecting an establishment of religion, or prohibiting the free exercise thereof . . ."

With these three constitutional references we have the sum and substance of the mandates. Each is absolute in its outreach. The religious test oath clause is unamendable. It simply says: Never! The First Amendment is almost as absolute: It says "no law."

But these guarantees, if sweeping, are also capable of many interpretations. For example, do the first ten words of the First Amendment call for a complete separation of church and state and, by implication, sectarian religion and public education? Those who favor this absolutist interpretation buttress it with the practical argument that to make any exception invites "the nose of the camel into the tent," "the foot in the door," and the "slippery slope" syndrome. Another school of interpreters concludes that the Constitution does not advocate a wall of separation between the religious and the secular, but rather only a prohibition on the establishment of a national religion and a preferential treatment of one sect over another.

As the Justices search for principled answers to perennial church-state questions, they often look beyond the Constitution and turn for additional guidance to a second major source of wisdom, the rich legacy of historical writings on church and state. When the nine Justices sit in their chambers and conference room weighing the meaning of these constitutional provisions, the ghosts of Roger Williams, Thomas Jefferson, James Madison and other colonial giants stalk the room and haunt their deliberations with whispered messages from a period rich with the claims of both the church and the state.

Justice Holmes once remarked that "A page of history is worth a volume of logic," an observation verified by a reading of the church-state cases. In the cases that follow, the references to history are many and varied, with the logic at times falling into the seductive category, rather than the deductive or inductive. In reading the historical record, each Justice marches to the tune of his own drummer, because history does not speak with mathematical certainty. The judicial use of the record of the colonial religious experience and the movement for disestablishment has evoked both criticism and defense of the Court, but the church-state literature is so valuable and the dilemmas so intractable that Justices will probably always look to the past in resolving the disputes of the present.

With this background in mind, let me try to provide some insight into the three religion clauses, taking them up in the order they appear in the Constitution and Bill of Rights. Given the extensive and complex nature of this area, what follows is but a panorama of the legal challenges and judicial responses.

34

Religious Test Oaths

As noted earlier, the prohibition of a religious test for public office in Article VI is the only substantive provision in the Constitution itself relating to religion. This clause was inserted into the document because the article requires that all federal officials take an oath to support the Constitution, and the framers wanted to guard against Congress adding a religious element to that oath.

According to nineteenth century Supreme Court Justice Joseph Story, the prohibition of a religious test was designed "to cut off forever every pretense of any alliance between church and state in the national government." That purpose is not surprising, since the framers of the Constitution themselves went to some lengths to keep religion separate from their deliberations. Not once did they engage in prayer during their four months together, and nowhere in the Constitution is there any invocation to God or acknowledgement of man's dependence on Him.

Article VI clearly prohibits religious oaths for federal office holders. The question for the Court was whether it had come to apply to state officials as well. The Maryland test oath case of 1961 offers us an unusual insight into the process of judicial decision-making because it shows how one issue can reach out and touch all three references to religion.

The Maryland Constitution provided that "No religious test ought ever to be required as a qualification for any office of profit or trust in this State, other than a declaration of belief in the existence of God . . ." A man named Torcaso had been appointed by the Governor to the office of Notary Public, but refused to take the oath and was denied his commission to serve. He appealed to the courts on the grounds that this oath violated Article VI of the United States Constitution and Amendments I and XIV.

Maryland's response was that a state had the power to impose criteria for its public office holders. In addition, the state took the position that no one is compelled to hold public office. The state courts upheld the state's position.

In deciding this case, the Supreme Court Justices could have based their decisions on any one of four grounds. First, they could have sided with Maryland, agreeing that the state could constitutionally prohibit those who wouldn't take the oath from holding office. If instead they sided with Torcaso, they could have chosen any of three rationales for applying the federal Constitution to this state requirement.

The key to each of these rationales is the Fourteenth Amendment. Since the 1920s, the U.S. Supreme Court has been incorporating provisions of the Bill of Rights (which applied initially only to the federal government) into the Due Process Clause of the Fourteenth Amendment (which applies to the states). At the time of this case, the First

Amendment had been incorporated completely, so that both Congress and the states could pass "no law respecting an establishment of religion, or prohibiting the free exercise thereof . . ."

Thus the Court could have ruled that the Maryland oath violated the First Amendment's wall of separation between church and state by establishing religion. They could have decided that the oath infringed on Torcaso's First Amendment right to believe or not to believe. Or they could have announced that Article VI applied to the states under the Fourteenth Amendment Due Process Clause.

Speaking for a unanimous Court, Justice Black declared the oath unconstitutional. He begins, not surprisingly, by turning to the pages of history. People, he says, came to this country "largely to escape religious test oaths." When they came here, however, one of the first things they did was to enact their own test oaths and to establish theocratic governments favorable to their own particular faiths.

And now comes the voice from the past. George Calvert, the first Lord Baltimore, one of the "wise and farseeing men in the Colonies," spoke out against this practice both in England and in the Colonies. It was his hope "to establish in Maryland a colonial government free from religious persecutions." It was these courageous dissenters who created the traditions which led to Article VI and Amendment I.

But on what grounds was the oath unconstitutional? If the Justices had decided to base their ruling on Article VI, they would have had to create a precedent by incorporating it into Amendment XIV, thus making it applicable to the states. If, however, the issue were decided under the First and Fourteenth Amendments, the Court would have no such problem because it would be following well-established precedents. So, the latter and easier route was taken and the Maryland law was declared to be unconstitutional because it invaded Torcaso's freedom of belief and religion guaranteed by Amendments I and XIV.

In a footnote Justice Black indicates that since the ruling is based on the First and Fourteenth Amendments, there is no need to consider Torcaso's argument that the Maryland oath also violated Article VI. This argument, nevertheless, seems to haunt the Justice and, in the following quotation, Black seems to indicate that the spirit of Article VI hovers over the case.

> We repeat and again reaffirm that neither a State nor the Federal Government can constitutionally force a person "to profess a belief or disbelief in any religion." Neither can they constitutionally pass laws or impose requirements which aid all religions as against nonbelievers, and neither can they aid those religions based on a belief in the existence of God as against

those religions founded on different belief.

As Justice Black points out, since there are groups in this country who do not profess a belief in the existence of God (Buddhism, Taoism, Ethical Culture, and Secular Humanism), the religious test oath discriminates against them too.

Establishment of Religion

Many of the most furious church-state battles have been fought over one form or another of alleged state preference to religion. This issue comes up repeatedly because, though no one religion predominates, ours is clearly a religious society. Examples of the pervasiveness of belief are all around us. Congress and our legislatures have refused to follow the example of the Constitutional Convention, preferring to begin their daily deliberations with prayer; a recent poll of high school student leaders found that only one percent classified themselves as atheists; a recent Gallup poll of voters found that heavy majorities would vote for a woman or a black or a member of any major religion as President, but most would not vote for an atheist.

Naturally, our laws sometimes reflect this omnipresence of religious belief, and it's the Supreme Court's job to determine whether these laws constitute "an establishment of religion" forbidden by the First Amendment.

Tax Exemption of Churches. Is it constitutional for a state to grant tax exemptions to religious organizations for properties which they use exclusively for religious worship? Isn't such an exemption a subsidy which aids in establishing religion? Aren't such tax exemption laws unconstitutional under the First and Fourteenth Amendments?

All 50 states (as well as the federal government) exempt places of worship from taxation. These laws and constitutional provisions were called into question in 1970, when the Supreme Court was asked to rule on a challenge to the New York State provision.

Unlike the brief unanimous decision of the Court in the Maryland test oath case, this ruling was considerably longer, with two concurring opinions and one dissent. Chief Justice Burger's opinion for the majority begins with the usual reference to the pages of history to show that a tradition of tax exemption goes back to colonial times and the early days of the Republic. Then, invoking familiar precedents, he concludes that history and past decisions support the conclusion that tax exemptions of religious organizations do not violate the Establishment Clause of the First Amendment as incorporated into the Due Process Clause of the Fourteenth.

Among the specific reasons given for the conclusion are:

There is neither advancement nor inhibition of religion in tax exemption. All religious groups are treated equally; there is no preferential treatment here and the churches are included with other charitable, scientific, professional, and patriotic groups in this exemption. In tax exemption the Government does not transfer funds, it simply refrains from demanding them. A state has the power to exempt from its taxation "certain entities that exist in harmonious relationship to the community at large," and that foster its "moral and mental improvement."

Justice Douglas was the sole dissenter. In his long years on the Court, his ideas on church-state relations changed greatly. He began by arguing that the state and religion should cooperate; he ended by insisting that the wall between church and state should be high and impregnable.

In a style characteristic of his later opinions, his dissent in the tax case brands the Court's ruling "a long step down the Establishment path." Why don't we, he asks, follow the Maryland oath case precedent condemning state and federal laws which aid believers against non-believers? By siding with believers against agnostics, atheists, and antitheological groups in its tax policies, he argues, the Court is throwing its weight behind an establishment of religion.

Never on Sunday. Many states have enacted Sunday closing laws, rooted in the religious tradition of "the Lord's Day" of church attendance and prayers. By this time such laws are becoming an anachronism, but their place in the church-state controversy is guaranteed by the issues they raise. Do they constitute an unconstitutional establishment of religion under the First and Fourteenth Amendments?

In 1961 the Supreme Court was called upon to decide four cases involving the constitutionality of the Sunday closing laws of Maryland, Massachusetts, and Pennsylvania. The complainants were employees of a discount store, the owners of a department store, and Orthodox Jews. The latter argued that their Sabbath day is Saturday and that they were disadvantaged religiously and economically by these laws, which established a tenet of the Christian religion. The others took the position that the Sunday closing laws were predominantly religious in nature, aimed at the constitutionally impermissible goal of encouraging church attendance and membership in the predominant Christian sects.

These four cases, with their majority, plurality, concurring, and dissenting opinions, wander all over the constitutional terrain. What emerges is a cacophony of voices agreeing that the laws in question are constitutional. The majority recognizes a growing secularization of what was once a spiritual experience. Sunday, in the eyes of the Justices, has become a day of rest, relaxation, and family togetherness. The state, in its wisdom, can decide to set aside Sunday to improve "the health, safety, recreation, and general well-being of our citizens."

Justice Douglas dissented in all four cases. He posed the issue as follows: "The question is whether a state can impose criminal sanctions on those who, unlike the Christian majority that makes up our society, worship on a different day or do not share the religious scruples of the majority." He answers in this way: "There is an 'establishment' of religion in the constitutional sense if any practice of any religious group has the sanction of law behind it."

Required Prayers and Bible Reading. With these cases we enter a terrain familiar to many people. In the tax-exemption and Sunday closing cases the Court decided that the challenged legislation did not unconstitutionally establish religion, but in these cases it ruled that school prayer did violate the Constitution by establishing religion. These decisions engendered a controversy that has not only continued to simmer but has led to a genteel type of lawlessness on the part of educators supported by community opinion.

In 1962 the Court declared unconstitutional the required recitation of the New York State Regents' prayer in the community of New Hyde Park. The 22-word nondenominational prayer was prepared by the Board of Regents as a way of developing moral and spiritual values in the school. By a six to one margin, the court ruled that the Board of Regents was not in the business of writing prayers for children. By doing so, it had violated the Establishment Clause of the First Amendment, as applied to the states through the Fourteenth Amendment.

One would have thought by the vociferous and vicious attacks on this ruling as atheistic and communistic that this was a sweeping indictment of prayers. Many of those who attacked the decision could not have read it with care.

The following year, the Court confronted squarely the issue of required prayers and sectarian Bible reading in the Pennsylvania and Maryland schools. This time, an eight to one decision outlawed these practices as enhancing religion and, thus, breaching the wall of separation. Five opinions were written, totaling 113 pages, in an attempt to answer the charges lodged against the Court the previous year.

In a key sentence, Justice Clark's opinion for the majority declares: "In the relationship between man and religion, the State is firmly committed to a position of neutrality." What this generalization actually means in practice will be seen in the cases which follow.

39

Public Aid for Parochial Schools and Colleges. Public assistance to the parochial schools is an issue that refuses to go away. Politically, it means votes; economically, it means direct or indirect financial assistance to hard-pressed religiously-oriented educational institutions; and socially, it offers parents and students a choice in education philosophies. No sooner do the courts declare a parochial law unconstitutional than, Phoenix-like, a new law rises to take its place — somewhat different and more ambitious and complex.

To summarize the cases and the nuances in the opinions would require an extended analysis. Instead, I'll focus on the options available to judges in resolving these sensitive issues.

Let us assume that a community decides to do the following:

Pay tax monies for bus transportation of public and parochial students in their schools; Buy with tax monies secular text-books which will be loaned to parochial schools; Use tax funds to defray part of the salaries of parochial school teachers; Provide parochial schools with such state-financed services as standardized tests and scoring assistance, therapeutic guidance, remedial services, field trips, and loan of instructional materials and equipment.

Are these forms of assistance constitutional under the Establishment Clause of the First Amendment as incorporated into the Fourteenth Amendment?

When these issues reached the United States Supreme Court, the Justices could follow any one of the several constitutional routes. There is the absolutist position advocated by Justice Rutledge, based on Madison's famous "Memorial and Remonstrance Against Religious Assessments," that the wall of separation is high and must not be breached.

At the other end of the continuum is the position that church and state are not adversaries, but partners in a common endeavor to foster good citizenship. So long as the state or federal assistance shows no preference for one religion over another, the legislation is constitutional.

A third option emerged in 1930 when Louisiana used tax monies to purchase secular books for parochial schools. It was challenged under the Fourteenth Amendment as an unconstitutional taking of private property for public use, rather than on the separation of state and church principle, but the issue is basically the same. The Court upheld the state's action as benefitting the child and the state, not the religion. This child benefit theory played a significant role in future rulings.

A fourth principle that has been advocated is that of neutrality — that is, the government must do nothing to aid or hinder religion. Over a period of time the Justices have clarified this approach to church-state issues by specifying certain guidelines by which legislation must be judged.

1. The purpose must be secular, not sectarian.
2. The primary effect must be neither to enhance nor hinder religion.
3. There must be no excessive entanglement between state and church.

With these guidelines the Court has approved bus transportation and loans of texts to parochial school students, as well as standardized tests for them and scoring, diagnostic, and therapeutic services. These services, however, must be performed by public school personnel or consultants hired by local school boards. No monies may be given directly to the parochial schools. The following laws were struck down: instructional equipment, field trip transportation, salaries for parochial school teachers, and tax benefits, as well as tuition reimbursements to parents who send their children to parochial schools.

The rationale for striking down some forms of aid and approving others is that the impermissible forms would benefit parochial education itself, rather than the child. In other words, the Court requires that the state not provide aid to the school (where it might contribute to religious education), but rather provide aid to children themselves and earmark it strictly for nonsectarian purposes.

This can be a hard distinction to draw, but in its most recent case on parochiaid the Court found that aid for guidance counseling is impermissible because helping parochial students select courses would inevitably involve the state in the day-to-day curriculum of the schools. It also struck down aid for field trip transportation because the schools would control the timing, frequency, and destination of the trips, so the aid would be to the school rather than to the children themselves.

But the Court has ruled that busing students to and from school is O.K. because parochial schools don't control such transportation, the transportation is not tied to specific learning activities, and the busing is part of the state's legitimate concern for the safety and well-being of all children. Similarly, speech, hearing, and psychological counseling is permissible because it isn't controlled by the school and is directly relevant to the child's well-being.

When it comes to church-related colleges and universities, the Justices tend to be more sympathetic to financial assistance. In approving federal grants for buildings to be used for libraries, music, arts, science, and language instruction, the Court in a five to four decision found the purpose to be secular, not sectarian. College students, declared the Court's opinion, are more sophisticated than their younger counterparts and, therefore, less easily indoctrinated. Also, there is no reason to suppose that sectarian dogma will intrude or be tolerated in secular instruction, where the spirit of academic freedom prevails.

One aspect of the law, however, was found to be unconstitutional. The provision that the buildings would revert to the college after 20 years made it possible for the college to use them for sectarian purposes. This was declared unacceptable under the Establishment Clause.

Freedom of Religion

Freedom of religion, the second of the religion clauses of the First Amendment, involves its own unique complexities. In its most simple connotation, it means the freedom to believe or not to believe. You and I have the right to be orthodox, agnostic, or atheist.

The complex constitutional confrontation takes place when the police power of the state demands conformity of an individual whose religion commands him to do something that puts him in conflict with the state. The specific instances can involve almost anything — from snake handling or peyote smoking during religious rituals to refusing blood transfusions — but the fundamental conflict is the same: the state invokes its power to protect the lives, health, morals, welfare, and safety of the community; the individual takes a stand on freedom of religion or conscience.

The Supreme Court cases move from the Mormons to Jehovah's Witnesses and the Amish, and from those who refuse to salute the flag to those who refuse to serve in the Armed Forces. They even encompass teaching about evolution in the school curriculum.

In the Mormon polygamy case of 1878, a unanimous Court turned a deaf ear to the plea of the Mormons that plural marriages were a religious obligation. Religious beliefs, proclaimed the Court, were protected by the First Amendment, but actions based on such beliefs were not immune from the arm of the law.

However, almost 100 years later, in 1972, the Court ruled that the beliefs of another group, the Amish, did justify them in not obeying the law. In this case, as in so many freedom of religion cases, the crux of the matter was not so much that sect members committed an overt criminal act (like taking plural wives), but rather that their religion compelled them to refrain from doing something that the law commanded. The Amish claimed that state law should not require them to send their children to public secondary school. A nearly unanimous Court agreed that the historic and venerable Amish had every right to protect the spiritual heritage which they hoped to pass on to their children from the secular influences of the public secondary school.

Justice Douglas, dissenting in part, wondered aloud whether this opinion of the Court is a step toward overruling the Mormon polygamy case, since in this instance a religious practice based on a religious belief was approved. By blunting the belief/action dichotomy of the Mormon case, the Court, he said, may be opening the door to a more sympathetic view of religious practices.

The Flag Salute Cases. The cases initiated by the sect known as Jehovah's Witnesses have done more than those of any other religious groups to probe the nature, scope, and limits of the principle of religious freedom. Between 1938 and 1943 they began 20 major cases before the Supreme Court, winning 14 of them.

The flag salute cases brought by the Jehovah's Witnesses provide one of the most intriguing examples of judicial reversal in the Court's entire history. In 1940, the Court was confronted by a suit claiming that a Pennsylvania requirement that the flag be saluted daily in public schools violated the religious freedom of the Jehovah's Witnesses, who were brought up to believe that such a gesture of respect for the flag was forbidden by scripture. The suit pitted freedom of conscience, protected by the First Amendment, against the state's authority to require school children to engage in patriotic exercises.

By an eight to one margin, the Court ruled in favor of the state. Justice Frankfurter, writing for the majority, ruled that religious liberty is an individual, precious right, but each citizen also has political responsibilities to the community which protects this and other rights. A state can require ceremonies for all children because "national unity is the basis for national security."

However, just three years later, the Court by a six to three margin struck down a West Virginia law that required all school children, including Jehovah's Witnesses, to salute the flag. Even though the nation was in the midst of a great war, and one might have thought that national unity was even more of an imperative, the Court determined that the individual's right of self-determination must be protected. Since the West Virginia law violated the sanctity of "the sphere of intellect and spirit which it is the purpose of the First Amendment to our Constitution to reserve from all official control," the Court declared the act unconstitutional.

Writing for the majority, Justice Robert Jackson pointed out that "Those who begin coercive elimination of dissent soon find themselves exterminating dissenters. Compulsory unification of opinion achieves only the unanimity of the graveyard." He pointed out that national unity, loyalty, and patriotism could be achieved in other ways than through compulsory flag salutes, and concluded with a passage that has become one of the most quoted in constitutional law:

If there is any fixed star in our constitutional constellation, it is that no official, high or petty, can prescribe what shall be orthodox in politics, nationalism, religion, or other matters of opinion. . . .

The Conscientious Objector Cases. In the second flag salute case the Court decided not only on the basis of religion but also on a broader concept, freedom of the intellect and spirit. This broader basis also underlies the conscientious objector cases of the Vietnam War, where there is implicit a concern for the importance of intellectual and spiritual freedom, even in time of national emergency.

Our country's draft laws have recognized the dilemmas posed by conscientious objectors, exempting those from combat whose "religious training and beliefs" prevent them from taking human life. Federal law has defined such belief as "an individual's relation to a Supreme Being involving duties superior to those arising from any human relation, but [not including] essentially political, sociological, or philosophical views or a merely personal moral code." By permitting conscientious objection on religious grounds but not for personal moral reasons, does the law unconstitutionally establish religion?

In 1965, the Court was confronted by three cases of young men who claimed conscientious objection but did not believe in God in the conventional sense. Did the law exempt only those who believe in an orthodox God, or could it encompass a broader faith?

In deciding the case, the Court was acutely aware of the religious diversity of a country with more than 250 sects and a vast range of views about a supernatural deity. The way out, a unanimous Court decided, was to formulate a rule of law covering this diversity of viewpoints, permitting young people to be exempted if they demonstrated "a sincere and meaningful belief which occupies in the life of its possessor a place parallel to that filled by God." Since these three men passed this test, they won their cases and were accorded CO status.

That decision did not resolve all difficult conscientious objector questions. Six years later, the Court was confronted by the cases of two young men who sought conscientious objector status because they objected not to all wars but to the Vietnam War in particular. The young men argued that limiting CO status to only those who opposed all wars violated the religion clauses of the First Amendment.

Not so, said the Court. The law didn't discriminate among religious groups, and so didn't contravene the prohibition against an establishment of religion. Although religious training or belief is required for exemption, no partisan creed or religious organization is singled out for special treatment.

One of the young men claimed that the Catholic religion taught him to distinguish between just and unjust wars. Didn't the law interfere with his freedom of religion and conscience? Once again the Court said no, finding no interference with any religious ritual or practice. If the law imposes an incidental burden to some young men, it is more than compensated for by the government's interest in obtaining manpower for the armed forces.

Never on Saturday? Several religions practiced in this country observe the Sabbath on a day other than Sunday. When their members try to observe their Sabbath, however, they often run into conflict with the law. The dispute over whether they are being deprived of their freedom of religion shows how the two religion clauses in the First Amendment are closely intertwined.

In 1965, the Court was confronted by the complaint of a Seventh-day Adventist, who claimed that she lost her job, as well as her unemployment insurance benefits, because her religion prohibited her from working on Saturday. She tried to get other employment, but failed because the plants in the community insisted on a six-day week. She was then denied unemployment benefits on the ground that she had failed to accept "suitable available work."

By a six to two margin, the Court upheld her right to unemployment benefits because she had been put to the "cruel choice" of choosing between her religion and her work. Justices Harlan and White dissented. Their ironic response is that the majority, by singling out a religious group for a special benefit, is contributing to an establishment of religion.

A recent case involved a member of the Worldwide Church of God, a Sabbatarian sect. When he was transferred to another building, he lost his seniority and was required to work on Saturday. He refused and was fired. He appealed under Title VII of the Civil Rights Act of 1964, which makes it unlawful employment practice for an employer to discriminate against an employee on the basis of religion. He also appealed under a guideline of the Equal Employment Opportunity Commission which requires an employer "to accommodate to the reasonable religious needs of employees . . . where such accommodation can be made without a serious inconvenience to the conduct of the business."

In a seven to two ruling, the Court upheld the company on the ground that it had done all that could be reasonably expected of it within the framework of the seniority system. But the two dissenters, Justices Marshall and Brennan, saw the majority opinion as an "ultimate tragedy" because it "seriously eroded our devotion to the principle of religious diversity." They went on to say: "All Americans will be a little poorer until today's decision is erased."

45

Teaching About Evolution. The Tennessee "monkey trial" of 1925 is the most famous judicial battle over whether the schools should teach a subject that offends a particular religion. Fundamentalists in Tennessee were instrumental in passing a law forbidding public schools "to teach the theory that denies the story of the divine creation of man as taught in the Bible." John Scopes, a young biology teacher, violated the law when he taught Darwin's theory of evolution. Critics scoffed that Darwin implied that man was descended from primates, so the press dubbed the case "the monkey trial."

The Scopes case featured the epic confrontation of two giants of the time: Clarence Darrow, the nation's most celebrated trial lawyer, defended Scopes and academic freedom; William Jennings Bryan, former U.S. Secretary of State and three-time nominee for President, was a special prosecutor for the state. Despite the legal fireworks, the result was a stand-off. Scopes was convicted by the trial court but the conviction was overturned on a technicality by the state supreme court.

In 1968, the Justices of the U.S. Supreme Court had the opportunity to decide a nearly similar case. An Arkansas law dating from the 20s forbade teaching the theory "that mankind ascended or descended from a lower order of animals." A Little Rock teacher challenged the law, and the Court agreed with her, trotting forth several reasons why the law offended the Constitution. Once again, the Court's thinking shows how closely related the First Amendment clauses are. '

Justice Fortas' opinion for the unanimous Court held that the law violated *both* religion clauses of the First Amendment, on the grounds that the two clauses have the joint goal of requiring government to be neutral between religion and religion, and between religion and nonreligion. Since the Arkansas law "cannot be defended as an act of religious neutrality," it must be struck down both as tending to establish a particular religious view and as tending to frustrate the free exercise of other views.

A concurring opinion by Justice Stewart added the weight of yet another First Amendment clause. He pointed out that the law was unconstitutional because it also violated the Amendment's guarantee of freedom of communication.

Clergy in Politics. Many states have provisions which attempt to assure the separation of church and state by disqualifying ministers from holding political office. Such laws have been challenged as infringing on the free exercise of religion, in effect pitting the two religion clauses of the First Amendment against each other.

In April of 1979, the Justices decided unanimously that a Tennessee law disqualifying ministers from serving as legislators was an unconstitutional infringement on freedom of religion. Chief Justice Burger wrote that the fatal defect in the law is that it conditions the right to free exercise of religion on the surrender of the right to hold public office.

Concluding Thoughts

The historic road from theocracy to disestablishment of religion and from religious intolerance to religious freedom has been long and tortuous. The American people and the courts have grappled with and will continue to encounter legislative policies and local customs bearing on the sensitive areas of the spiritual and the secular. In addition to the issues discussed above, the courts have been involved in released time mandates, religious proselytizing, and ecclesiastical controversies involving church governance. There is no dearth of problems.

Nor is there any one way of settling conclusively all the issues. As we indicated in the opening quotes from Justices Rutledge and Douglas, the absolutist principle of separation of church and state will be countered with the contention that we are a religious people and that the church and state are not adversaries, but partners in the democratic adventure. On this continuum of opposing positions, judges will strive to formulate principles that either accommodate the two or accentuate the polarities. The resolution of these soul-searching and mind-perplexing controversies is of great consequence to every American. In this matter, to paraphrase Abraham Lincoln, no one is a bystander.

[Editor's note: In the following article, written in 1985, Professor Starr examines how the Supreme Court has interpreted the religion clauses of the First Amendment since 1979.]

MY PILGRIMAGE
TO THE WALL OF SEPARATION
. . .

Periodically, I make my pilgrimage to the Wall of Separation. By this time, the scene is a familiar one. The Nine Guardians are sitting atop the Wall listening to the pleadings below: raise the Wall, lower it, fill in the gaping holes, and look, it is not really a wall, it's only a figure of speech.

Responding to these pleas, the Guardians have posted along The Wall many judicial pronouncements which, in turn, have evoked such graffiti as:

I think that it is important for us, if we're going to maintain our constitutional principles, that we support Supreme Court decisions even when we may not agree with them.

— John F. Kennedy

47

We're in a bad fix in America when eight evil old men and a vain and foolish woman can speak a verdict on American liberties.
— Rev. Bob Jones III

My last visit was in 1979 when I found The Wall in pretty good shape. Now a new cast of actors has appeared in the pleadings, with the President of the United States in the starring role. President Reagan's plea to the American people, in general, and to the Congress and the Supreme Court, in particular, is to restore traditional American values, with special emphasis on prayers in the public schools, public financial assistance to parents who send their children to private and parochial schools, and equal access of religious groups to public school facilities.

Are the Guardians listening? Let us see.

The Ground Rules

The Constitution contains the commandment that "no religious Test shall ever be required as a Qualification to an Office or public Trust under the United States." Since this means *never*, this is one of the provisions of the Constitution which cannot be amended. It is a point of historical interest that this command is rarely invoked to discern the thoughts of the Founding Fathers on the role of religion in government.

The second commandment in the Constitution relating to religion is found in the first sixteen words of the First Amendment: "Congress shall make no law respecting an establishment of religion, or prohibiting the free exercise thereof . . ." The first ten words are referred to as the Establishment Clause and the remainder as the Free Exercise Clause.

Often these two clauses are invoked against each other. For example, there are those who argue that their freedom to exercise their religion extends to the classrooms of the public schools. Their opponents counter that the Establishment Clause has priority because it sets up a wall of separation between church and state (Jefferson's famous metaphor) and negates practices in the public schools. A second example of these two constitutional clauses on a collision course deals with an individual who is transferred in his plant to work in the armaments division. He refuses because of his religious beliefs, and he leaves his job and requests unemployment insurance. If the state grants his request, is it aiding in an establishment of religion? There are, of course, numerous other examples, as we shall see.

Although the two religion clauses of the First Amendment are a limitation on the powers of Congress, the Supreme Court has decided in a number of rulings that they are also binding on the states. The Court has used the Fourteenth Amendment's mandate that no state shall deprive a person of liberty without due process of law as the basis for the

48

extension of the principles. This interpretation of the Fourteenth Amendment has not gone unchallenged by those who accuse the Court of judicial legislation or judicial activism run riot.

In interpreting the thinking behind the religion clauses, two schools have taken center stage in recent years: the Separatists and the Accommodationists. Neither school is monolithic in its views, and there are gradations of opinion. In general, however, the Separatists would like to see a high and impregnable wall, while the Accommodationists believe that the Framers were opposed only to a national religion and the preference of one religious group over another. They take the position that in all other respects the Framers intended no hostility toward religion because they respected traditional religious values.

In grappling with the contemporary contending positions of the Separatists and the Accommodationists, as well as with the historical record, the Justices have formulated a guideline in *Lemon v. Kurtzman,* 91 S. Ct. 2105 (1971), which they tend to follow, even though some of them protest regularly that they are not bound by any hard and fast rules. Chief Justice Burger wrote the opinion in that case, in which he declared that in Establishment Clause cases a governmental law or conduct will be held to be constitutional only if it meets all of the following three criteria:

1. The purpose of the law or conduct must be secular, not sectarian.
2. The principal or primary effect of the law or conduct must be neither to advance nor inhibit religion.
3. The act or conduct must not create an excessive governmental entanglement with religion.

As will be seen in the cases which follow, the Justices tend at times to invoke a second guideline, which is referred to as the strict scrutiny rule. When this is done, the Justices require the national or state governments to show a *compelling interest* to justify any legislation or conduct which impinges on religious beliefs and practices. In addition to this requirement, the government must also show to the satisfaction of a majority of the Justices that they used the least restrictive measures in dealing with religious matters.

A third guideline which the Court followed in past parochiaid cases but seems to have dropped for the time being is the child benefit test. This idea was used to justify appropriating public funds to reimburse parents who bused their children to parochial school and, in addition, to support lending secular textbooks purchased with public funds to parochial schools.

An especially interesting feature of all religious cases is the invocation of Clio, the muse of history, as an expert witness for each side. As expert witnesses go, Clio, like Janus, can face in opposite directions at the same time.

Creches Attain Tenure

The Christmas season, with its secular holiday from work and its sectarian call to worship, also brings with it nativity scene confrontations. Especially in recent years, cities, as well as the national government, find themselves enmeshed in controversies which lay claim to historic customs and traditions, constitutional principles, and community practices.

Is it constitutional when a government purchases a creche and erects it on privately owned land during the Christmas season? Does it make a constitutional difference if the creche is owned by a private group but displayed in a public park? The following two cases explore these issues.

The Rhode Island Creche Case. For forty years, the city of Pawtucket, Rhode Island, had erected a Christmas display in a privately owned part in the downtown business sector. This observance of the holiday season included a nativity scene in addition to the usual ornaments: reindeer, Christmas tree, Santa Claus house, sleigh, animals, and a large banner proclaiming "Season's Greetings."

The city had originally purchased the creche, which was now worth about $200. It cost the city $20 to erect and to dismantle the creche and a nominal expense in lighting the scene.

Pawtucket residents and the local affiliate of the American Civil Liberties Union challenged the constitutionality of the creche on the ground that it violated the Establishment Clause of the First Amendment, which is binding on the state under the Fourteenth Amendment. The city lost in the federal district court, and in the court of appeals, taking its case to the Supreme Court in Lynch v. Donnelly, 104 S. Ct. 1355 (1984). The government of the United States submitted an amicus curiae brief on behalf of the city.

To read the opinions of the majority and minority is to sense that the debate among the Justices was intense. What is especially interesting about the opinions is their appeal to history to undergird their positions.

Writing for the majority, Chief Justice Burger emphasizes that the nativity scene, commemorating "a particular historic religious event," has been recognized in the western world for twenty centuries and in our country for two centuries. The Chief Justice reasons that our nation has always recognized the pervasiveness of religious belief. For example, in the very week that Congress adopted the Establishment Clause in the

50

Bill of Rights, it passed a law providing for paid chaplains in the House and Senate to conduct prayers. Some of our national holidays, such as Thanksgiving and Christmas, have their origins in religious practices. Public employees are paid out of public funds, even though they do not work on these days. "In God We Trust" and "One Nation Under God" are additional examples of the government accommodating its policies to religious beliefs and practices. Our motto as a nation, says the Chief Justice, is "accommodation of all faiths and all forms of religious expression and hostility toward none."

Justice Brennan, writing for himself and the other dissenters (Justices Marshall, Blackmun, and Stevens), offers his own version of the uses of history in judicial reasoning. The mere fact that a particular practice has been around for a long time does not give it constitutional tenure. In addition, he points out, Justice Burger has not researched adequately the particular religious practice that is central to this case. In colonial days, there was widespread hostility to the celebration of Christmas as a "Popish" practice. Some sects incorporated Christmas in their celebrations; others did not. This deeply divisive matter was not resolved until the middle of the nineteenth century, when some states and the national government gave public recognition to Christmas by declaring it a public holiday. The creche itself seems to have been introduced by German immigrants in the early eighteenth century, and it was not until the twentieth century that its use became widespread.

Justice Brennan then summarizes his view of the majority's use of history.

> In sum, there is no evidence whatsoever that the Framers would have expressly approved a federal celebration of the Christmas holiday including public displays of a nativity scene. . . . Nor is there any suggestion that publicly financed and supported displays of Christmas creches are supported by a record of widespread, undeviating acceptance that extends throughout our history. . . . Contrary to today's careless decision . . . the "illumination" provided by history must always be focused on the particular practice at issue in a given case. Without that guiding principle and the intellectual discipline it imposes, the Court is at sea, free to select random elements of America's varied history solely to suit the views of five members of this Court.

In turning from history to the law in the case, Chief Justice Burger, speaking for the majority of five, condemns an absolutist approach as simplistic. Total separation of church and state is impossible because religion is intertwined in the fabric of American cultural and political life. The Founding Fathers intended accommodation toward religion, not hostility, and presidential proclamations and congressional practices attest to "acknowledgment of our religious heritage."

In applying the *Lemon* criteria, the Chief Justice concludes that the nativity scene is constitutional. As to the first criterion, the creche, he says, must be viewed "in the context of the Christmas season," and, as such, the entire display was secular in its objective. Its purpose was to celebrate a national holiday, and the creche simply focused attention on the historical origins of this traditional observance. There was nothing in the display that indicated Pawtucket's support for Christianity or hostility or disapproval of other religions.

The Chief Justice also finds that the creche meets the second *Lemon* criterion. The display did not have as its primary effect the endorsement or disapproval of religion. The benefit to the Christian faith in this display of the secular and the sectarian is "indirect, remote, and incidental."

Finally, there was no excessive entanglement—the third criterion—between church and state. The governmental expenditure to maintain the display was minimal and there was no church intervention. Nor was there evidence of political divisiveness or political friction over the creche during the forty years of its tenure.

But wasn't the display designed really to serve commercial interests and to bring shoppers into the central city? Why was it necessary to include the creche? Chief Justice Burger answers that it serves as a reminder of the religious origin of the holiday. It is a "passive symbol," like a religious painting, which should cause no offense.

Justice Brennan's dissent invokes the three *Lemon* criteria with different results. He finds the creche a sectarian intrusion into a secular exhibit. With the exception of the creche, the display used traditional secular figures to attract people into the downtown area in order to promote preholiday sales. The nativity scene introduced a distinctively religious element, which served a distinctively sectarian purpose. The record in the district courts showed that the city government reflected the views of the majority that it is a "good thing" to "keep Christ in Christmas."

The primary effect of the nativity scene was to aid the dominant religious group at the expense of the minority. Christianity was singled out for special treatment. "It was precisely this sort of religious chauvinism," says the Justice, "that the Establishment Clause was intended forever to prohibit."

As for excessive entanglement between church and state, it is evident that much has happened since the inception of this case. Since the mayor has promised the Jews to include a Menorah in future displays, it is reasonable to anticipate that other religious groups will make similar demands. What limits will there be on accommodation? As the Justice notes, religious differences generate powerful emotional reactions, and the result does not bode well for future controversies of this nature.

Justice O'Connor wrote a concurring opinion in which she agreed with the majority that the display did not represent an endorsement or disapproval of religion. It was simply a traditional symbol used in a secular setting to celebrate an important public holiday.

Justice Blackmun wrote a separate dissenting opinion, in which Justice Stevens joined. He warns that the city has won a Pyrrhic victory because the creche "has been relegated to the role of a neutral harbinger of the holiday season, useful for commercial purposes, but devoid of any inherent meaning and incapable of enhancing the religious tenor of a display of which it is an integral part . . . This is a misuse of a sacred symbol."

The Scarsdale (New York) Creche Case. The Scarsdale case differed from the Pawtucket case in several respects. In the Pawtucket case, as we have seen, a publicly owned Christmas exhibit which included a creche had been displayed on privately owned property in the center of the business district for forty years. In the Scarsdale case, a group of citizens had been displaying a privately owned creche in a public park where celebrations of Christmas had been held for twenty-five years. Do these factual differences constitute constitutional difference?

The village of Scarsdale had no specific ordinance relating to the use of its public parks and no standards for granting or denying permission. The governing board permitted its parks to be used for demonstrations, speeches, silent vigils, and the distribution of petitions. In 1956, the board was asked by and granted permission to the Creche Committee, a private organization of Catholic and Protestant churches, to place a creche in Boniface Circle, a public park, during the 1957 Christmas season. These requests continued until 1982 and were granted, at first with unanimous approval. Beginning in 1973, there was a gradual escalation of disapproval on the board, with minority votes or abstentions. Suggestions were made by the mayor and others that in the future the creche be placed on private property. When the board voted 4 to 3 to deny the Creche Committee's request for 1982, the issue was joined in the United States district court. At this time the Pawtucket case had not been decided by the United States Supreme Court.

In its thorough opinion, the district court ruled that Boniface Circle was a traditional public forum. As such, it was open to all types of speech — religious and nonreligious. On the precedent of the Widmar case (equal access of college students, discussed below), the court noted that a government cannot normally deny access to public forums based on the content of speech. Such content-based denials usually violate the Free Speech Clause of the First Amendment as applied to the states under the Fourteenth Amendment. However, declared the court, in this instance Scarsdale had a compelling state interest to avoid violating the Establishment Clause. Scarsdale won, and the Creche Committee appealed.

Before the appellate court, Scarsdale took the position that the village must be nonpartisan in religious matters; that its park was not a public forum for disseminating sectarian or partisan positions; that alternative private sites were available to the Creche Committee; and that, unlike the Pawtucket case, the issue here involved a privately owned creche and a public park, not a publicly owned creche in a private park. Since many in the Scarsdale community were conscientiously opposed to the display, argued Scarsdale, the controversy generated divisive political confrontations which have led to excessive entanglement between church and government.

The Creche Committee say it differently. Using the Widmar equal access case, it argued that the creche display was protected by the First Amendment. The display was an example of religious speech, and since Scarsdale had no ordinance limiting public displays in its public parks, there was no compelling governmental reason for it to discriminate against this type of speech.

By the time the United States Court of Appeals decided the case, the Supreme Court had handed down its Pawtucket ruling. Would it make a difference?

The issue here, said the appeals court, is reconciling the Establishment Clause with the Free Speech Clause of the First Amendment, *McCreary v. Stone,* 739 F.2d 716 (1984). With these two important rights on a collision course, one way to resolve the dilemma is to subject the facts in the case to the *Lemon* criteria. The three appellate judges agreed with the district court judge that the secular purpose prong had been met. By accommodating a privately owned creche in a public park that is a traditional public forum, Scarsdale was not engaged in any sectarian activity.

Would Scarsdale's permission to exhibit the creche advance religion? No, said the court, because Scarsdale's role was only "indirect, remote, and incidental" so far as aid to religion was involved. The prestige, power, and influence of the village were nowhere evident. As a matter of fact, since 1976 a disclaimer sign had been required as a condition for the authorization to display the creche which read: "This creche has been erected and maintained solely by the Scarsdale Creche Committee, a private organization."

Was there excessive entanglement between government and religion? No, replied the judges, because no subsidies were involved and potential or future political divisiveness cannot invalidate an otherwise permissible display.

An interesting sidelight in the court's ruling is the discussion of the size of the disclaimer sign. The district court judge took the position that children viewing the creche might conclude that the village supported the religious symbol. Although the appeals court found little evidence to support this conclusion, it did instruct the lower court to see to it that future signs will be sufficiently large and visible so that the disclaimer can be clearly seen and read.

Obviously, the Pawtucket case had made a difference. Scarsdale lost. It then turned to the court of last resort.

On appeal to the Supreme Court of the United States, Scarsdale lost again, this time on a 4 to 4 vote. On March 27, 1985 in *McCreary v. Stone,* the divided Court upheld the appeals court in a one-sentence ruling. There was no opinion, nor any indication as to how the Justices voted, although one might infer from the Pawtucket case how they stood on the issues. Justice Powell, who had missed the hearing because of surgery, did not participate.

Chaplains Are In: Politics And Prayer

James Kilpatrick remarked in one of his columns that 200 years of tradition count for more than the three-part *Lemon* test. This was true in the Pawtucket and Scarsdale creche cases and, as we shall see, it carried weight in the Nebraska chaplain case, *Marsh v. Chambers,* 103 S. Ct. 3330 (1983).

Like most state lawmaking bodies, the Nebraska legislature begins each session with a prayer offered by a chaplain paid out of public funds. Since 1965, their chaplain has been the same Presbyterian minister, who is paid a monthly stipend for each month the legislature is in session. Chambers, a member of the legislature and a Nebraska taxpayer, protested the practice as a violation of the Establishment Clause.

Chief Justice Burger begins his opinion for the majority by confessing that "historical patterns cannot justify contemporary violations of constitutional guarantees." Having said this, he immediately launches into the historical background of the "unique history" of the issue before the Court.

He takes the position that two centuries of national practice and one century of state practice call for judicial notice and respect. He notes that the practice of opening legislative sessions with prayers is deeply embedded in "the history and traditions of this country." Although the Constitutional Convention did not open with a prayer (was it Hamilton who objected to invoking the assistance of an alien power?), both houses of the first Congress agreed to have paid chaplains open their sessions with prayers. Since three days later this same Congress reached final agreement on the wording of the First Amendment, it is reasonable to infer, he concludes, that the Framers of the Bill of Rights saw no conflict between legislative prayers and the First Amendment.

What we have here, declares Chief Justice Burger, is "simply a tolerable acknowledgment of beliefs widely held among the people of the country." The prayers, a part of the fabric of American society, have become embedded in the history and tradition of this country, and cannot be construed as a "proselytizing activity." Legislators are adults who, unlike the young, are not susceptible to religious indoctrination.

Granting that this religious exercise has been secularized by historic tradition and custom, doesn't this practice violate the other tenets of the *Lemon* guidelines? For example, a clergyman from one Christian denomination has presided for sixteen years and his prayers have been rooted in the Judeo-Christian religion. Doesn't this practice aid religion? No, replies the Chief Justice, because there is no evidence of proselytizing on behalf of one faith and the disparagement of others. The chosen chaplain apparently was acceptable to the legislature "because of his performance and personal qualities." In addition guest chaplains were used on occasion.

The Chief Justice goes on to reassure us that there is no real threat to the Establishment Clause "while this Court sits." We shall see.

Writing for himself and Justice Marshall, Justice Brennan asks: What happened to the Lemon criteria? Why didn't the majority truly apply them? Was it because such application might prove fatal to their position?

Applying the *Lemon* criteria, he finds that the practice of paid chaplains violates the letter and spirit of the Establishment Clause. In the first place, the purpose of the prayer is primarily religious, not secular. To claim a secular purpose for a religious prayer is an insult to those who believe seriously in invoking Divine guidance. If, on the other hand, the purpose of the prayer is to get the legislators to quiet down and to inspire them to high purpose, surely, suggests the Justice, there are secular means available for that purpose.

In the second place, the primary effect of legislative prayers is "to impose indirect coercive pressure upon religious minorities to conform to the prevailing officially approved religion. The prayer creates "a linkage of religious beliefs and state power resulting in a symbolic benefit to religion."

Finally, the practice leads to excessive governmental entanglement with religion. Choosing a chaplain and monitoring his voluntary prayers is entanglement. Differences between the Nebraska legislator and his colleagues over the practice, as well as differences over the content of some of the prayers, has introduced unacceptable political divisiveness over religious matters.

Justice Brennan concludes with a shot that must have left a wound or two.

> In sum, I have no doubt that, if any group of law students were asked to apply the principles of *Lemon* to the question of legislative prayers, they would nearly unanimously find the practice to be unconstitutional.

Not satisfied with observation about the majority's lack of skill in applying the *Lemon* guidelines, he then takes them to task for their "betrayal of the lessons of history." The Framers of the First Amendment may have approved prayers in both houses of Congress because of "the passions and exigencies of the moment." The bandwagon effect of the moment was repudiated by Madison, when he had time to reflect in later life. The Constitution is not a static document, observes the Justice, and to be truly faithful to the Framers, the "uses of the history of their time must limit itself to broad purposes." The two foundation stones of the Establishment Clause are separation of church and state and neutrality in matters of religious doctrine and practices. Prayer is religious worship and it belongs in the private domain.

The brief dissent by Justice Stevens concludes that the long tenure of the official chaplain in this case is evidence of religious preference in violation of the Establishment Clause. What the majority has failed to do is to "parse" the content of some of the prayers given by the chaplain. Had they done so, they would have found clearly sectarian invocations unacceptable under the First Amendment. Is his tenure, asks the Justice, in some way related to the approval of this content by the majority of the legislators?

The Decalogue is Out

The Ten Commandments have been with us for thousands of years, much longer than nativity scenes and legislative prayers. However, when Kentucky tried to post the Decalogue in the classrooms of the public schools, the Court refused to grant this historic document tenure.

In 1978, Kentucky passed a law requiring the posting of the Ten Commandments in each public classroom. At the bottom of each display was a religious disclaimer: "The secular application of the Ten Commandments is clearly seen in its adoption as the fundamental legal code of Western Civilization and the common law of the United States." The copies were purchased with private contributions.

The state trial court sustained the statute under the *Lemon* criteria, and the state supreme court affirmed by an equally divided vote.

The Supreme Court of the United States granted *certiorari* and decided the case on the record without oral argument, *Stone v. Graham,* 101 S. Ct. 192 (1980). In a 5 to 4 per curiam opinion, it overruled both Kentucky courts and held this practice to be a violation of the first criterion of the *Lemon* guidelines. The purpose of posting the commandments, declared the majority, cannot be construed as secular, even though the state says so. "The Ten Commandments," emphasizes the opinion, "are undeniably a sacred text in the Jewish and Christian faiths, and no legislative recitation of a supposedly secular purpose can blind us to that fact."

It would be another matter if the commandments were integrated into the school curriculum, "where the Bible may constitutionally be used in an appropriate study of history, civilization, ethics, comparative religion, or the like." In this case, however, the mere posting served no such educational purpose. Quite the contrary, it might encourage students "to read, meditate upon, perhaps to venerate and obey, the commandments." This is not permissible under the Establishment Clause.

The fact that voluntary private contributions were involved does not change the constitutional implications. What is determinative of the issue is the posting under the auspices of the state legislature.

The Chief Justice and Justice Blackmun dissented on the ground that the Court should have accorded this case the treatment it deserved. Instead of a summary reversal, the parties should have been accorded a full-scale hearing before the Court. Justice Stewart agreed and indicated that, in his judgment, the Kentucky courts had applied the correct constitutional criteria.

In contrast to the brief three and four line dissenting comments of his brethren, Justice Rehnquist elaborated on his disagreement with the majority. In Establishment Clause cases, he points out, the Court as a rule looks to "legislative articulation of a statute's purpose." The majority's rejection of the state's declared secular purpose — accepted by the state courts — "is without precedent in Establishment jurisprudence." The fact that the Ten Commandments include secular and religious provisions does not render the law unconstitutional.

Justice Rehnquist agrees with the Kentucky legislature that this historic document has had an important influence on the development of the legal codes of the western world. It is impossible to insulate from the public sector the many aspects of our lives which have their origins in religion. After all, "religion has been closely identified with our history and government" and "the history of man is inseparable from the history of religion." He concludes by condemning the Court's summary reversal of Kentucky's highest court as "cavalier."

If You Don't Succeed, Try, Try Again!

For years, supporters of public financial aid to parochial schools have been searching for a magic formula to win over the Supreme Court to their position. In the *Everson* case (67 S. Ct. 504, 1947), they won reimbursement for transportation costs in busing their children to public schools. In the *Allen* case (88 S. Ct. 1923, 1968), they succeeded in persuading the Court to uphold the New York state law authorizing the loan of textbooks purchased with public funds to parochial schools, as well as public schools.

They lost, however, when they tried to obtain state financial assistance to supplement teachers' salaries in parochial schools. Nor did they succeed when the Court struck down a New York state law providing for tuition reimbursement and a tax relief program for those who sent their children to parochial schools, *Committee for Public Education and Religious Liberty v. Nyquist,* 93 S. Ct. 2955 (1973).

They finally seem to have found the formula in the Minnesota law which permits parents of *public and parochial* students, in computing their income taxes, to deduct from gross income expenses incurred in providing "tuition, textbooks and transportation." Deductions were limited to $500 per child in grades K-6 and $700 in grades 7-12.

Two facts are worth noting. Of the 820,000 students attending school in Minnesota, 91,000 attended private schools. Of these, 95% were enrolled in parochial schools. The second fact is that the lower courts, in interpreting the nature of "tuition, textbooks, and transportation" deductions, included summer-school tuition, Montessori School tuition (K-12), the cost of tennis shoes and sweat shirts for physical education, costs of pencils and special notebooks, rental fees for cameras and musical instruments, and costs of supplies needed in special classes.

Does this law violate the *Lemon* three-part test? We have in *Mueller v. Allen,* 103 S. Ct. 3062 (1983), another 5 to 4 donnybrook.

Writing for the majority, Justice Rehnquist finds that the Minnesota law meets all criteria of the *Lemon* guidelines. It has a secular legislative purpose because it applies to all educational expenses incurred by parents who send their children to public and parochial schools. He argues as follows:

An educated populace is essential to the political and economic health of any community, and a state's efforts to assist parents in meeting the rising cost of educational expenses plainly serves this secular purpose of ensuring that the state's citizenry is well-educated. Similarly, Minnesota, like other states, could conclude that there is a strong public interest in assuring the continued financial health of private schools, both sectarian and non-sectarian. By educating a substantial number of students, such schools relieve public schools of a corresponding great burden — to the benefit of all taxpayers. In addition, private schools may serve as a benchmark for public schools, in a manner analogous to the "TVA yardstick" for private power companies.

In the second place, the Minnesota statute does not have the primary effect of advancing the sectarianism of the parochial schools. The pivotal point is that the deduction is available to *all parents* who send their children to school, whether public, private, or parochial. In deciding on tax deductions, legislatures have wide latitude, and the deduction in this case is comparable to medical and charitable expenditures. An additional constitutional consideration is that the aid in this case is directed to the parents and not to the schools.

To the contention that the law was aimed directly at aiding sectarian schools because most public school parents do not pay tuition while the other deductible expenses are negligible compared to the benefits derived by parochial school beneficiaries, Justice Rehnquist seems to say that statistical evidence cannot be used to determine the constitutionality of this type of legislation. What seems to be controlling here is that parochial schools provide wholesome competition through an educational alternative. In addition, "they relieve substantially the tax burden incident to the operation of the public schools."

Finally, Justice Rehnquist concludes that the Minnesota law does not involve the state in excessive entanglement with religion. State supervision of the selection of textbooks for parochial schools to determine which ones do not qualify for deduction creates no problem for experienced educators.

Justice Marshall wrote the dissent, in which Justices Brennan, Blackmun, and Stevens joined. The opinion wastes no time in branding the Minnesota law as a violation of the Establishment Clause. What a state cannot do directly, warns the Justice, it cannot do indirectly. What the Nyquist decision had outlawed in 1973 (direct grants to parochial schools or tax benefits to parents of parochial school children), Minnesota cannot reinstate. By whatever name you call it, whether "tax credit" or "tax deduction," what we have here is "a subsidy of tuition masquerading as a subsidy of general educational expenses."

Justice Marshall is willing to grant that the law in question serves a secular purpose. It can promote "pluralism and diversity among the

State's public and nonpublic schools." But the law fails the constitutional test because its primary purpose is to aid sectarian education by subsidizing tuition payments. It has "a direct and immediate effect of advancing religion."

As for the majority's qualms about using statistical evidence to measure the impact of legislation, Justice Marshall sees no reason why empirical data should be avoided. His assessment of the situation is that in 1978-1979 the parents of the 91,000 students attending nonpublic schools charging tuition were entitled to the tax deduction. At the same time, only 79 public school students paid tuition because they went to schools outside their district. That meant that the parents of the other 815,000 students who attended public schools were not entitled to receive the tax benefit. With tongue in cheek, Justice Marshall suggests that the latter can obtain full tax benefits, if they can buy $700 worth of pencils, notebooks, and bus rides for their children.

Although on its face the Minnesota law grants tax deductions to parents of public and nonpublic students for certain specified expenditures, Marshall writes that the impact of the law is to offer an incentive to send children to parochial school, and it requires the taxpayers in general to pay for the cost of parochial education.

Another Parochiaid Victory

The tactic of trying again if you don't succeed also proved successful in a prior case and may become the strategy of the future. When the Supreme Court nullified in the 1073 *Nyquist* case, a New York state law providing reimbursement to parochial schools for expenses of tests and examinations, New York tried again and won in 1980 in *Committee for Public Education v. Reagan*, 100 S. Ct. 840 (1980).

The later attempt authorized cash payments to private and parochial schools as reimbursement for performing certain testing and reporting services mandated by a new state law. The services which were compensated were grading of state-prepared examinations by parochial school personnel and annual reports relating to the student body, the faculty, support staff, physical facilities, and the curriculum of each school.

The New York law barely survived in a 5 to 4 confrontation. Justice White wrote the majority opinion, concluding that there is nothing in the *Lemon* criteria to cast the pall of unconstitutionality on this legislation. The purpose of the testing, record keeping, and reporting is secular and related to the state's educational goals. Any religious intervention is minimal, since the state education department can review the procedures. The fact that the state is paying for these services of the parochial school faculty does not invoke the specter of excessive entanglement.

The state is required to audit the services, and it can be trusted to detect any deviance from the secular mandate of the law. There is no need, declares Justice White, to impute bad faith, nor is there any basis for concluding that the funds will be used to enhance religion.

Somewhat troubled, however, by the attack of the minority, Justice White concedes that cases in this murky area do not furnish "a litmus-paper test to distinguish permissible from impermissible aid to religiously oriented schools." The Court, he concludes, will have to muddle along from case to case until it finds a "more encompassing construction of the Establishment Clause."

Justice Blackmun, speaking for Justices Brennan and Marshall, accuses the majority of "taking a long step backwards" in the continuing controversy over providing public aid to parochial schools. Agreeing that the purpose of the New York statute is secular, he concludes that the direct subsidy aids religion by covering some of the operating costs of the sectarian school and, in this way, aids the school as a whole. The excessive entanglement criterion is also involved here because, to make certain that the public funds are not used for religious purposes, the state is obligated to engage in "ongoing surveillance."

Justice Stevens wrote his own dissent, charging that the majority approval of the direct subsidy to parochial schools opens a Pandora's box of possible future expenditures to reimburse staff for conducting fire drills or for constructing fireproof premises. He concludes his very brief opinion with these words.

> Rather than continuing with the Sisyphean task of trying to patch together the "blurred, indistinct, and variable barrier," . . . I would resurrect the "high and impregnable wall" between church and state constructed by the Framers of the First Amendment.

The asides, or to use that old-fashioned phrase "obiter dicta," of Justices White and Stevens convey the frustration that inheres in trying to wend one's constitutional way through the tortuous path of church-state relationships.

Parochiaid — No!

Technically, the next case does not fall within the traditional category of parochiaid. In reality, however, since it deals with tax exemption for sectarian institutions, it does come within the umbrella of public aid to religious schools and colleges.

Prior to 1970, the Internal Revenue Service (IRS) had interpreted the Internal Revenue Code as extending tax exemption to private schools, even to those which discriminated in their admissions policy against blacks. Tax exemption relieved the institutions from the payment of Social Security and unemployment taxes, and it treated gifts to the schools as charitable deductions. A group of black Mississippi parents and students challenged this policy in federal courts, and the IRS reversed itself. This new policy was upheld by the federal court and affirmed by the Supreme Court without opinion.

Under this new policy, tax exemption was denied to both Bob Jones University and to the Goldsboro Christian Schools because of their discrimination against blacks. Both institutions appealed to the courts and lost.

In January 1982, the IRS reversed itself again, because of pressure from the Reagan Administration, which took the position that tax exemption in these cases was the business of Congress and not within the jurisdiction of the IRS. Confronted with widespread public protests, the Administration announced that it would ask Congress to empower the IRS to deny tax exemption to institutions which discriminate on racial grounds. Congress did not act, but the court of appeals prohibited granting an exemption to the two institutions and they appealed their case to the Supreme Court.

In arguing their cases before the High Court, both institutions appealed to the Free Exercise of Religion Clause of the First Amendment. The Goldsboro Schools maintained that their interpretation of the Bible required them to exclude non-Caucasians from their institutions. Bob Jones University contended that its policy was no longer discriminatory. It now allowed all races to enroll with the stipulation that there must be no interracial dating or marriages or advocacy of such practices.

Bob Jones University also invoked the Establishment Clause on the ground that the IRS action against it preferred religions which do not discriminate racially over those which believe that the Bible forbids racial intermarriage.

In its 7 to 1 ruling in *Bob Jones University v. United States,* 76 L. Ed. 2d 157 (1983), the Supreme Court enunciated the principle that sincerely held religious beliefs do not justify practices which contravene public policy proclaimed in congressional enactments, judicial rulings, and Executive Orders. Writing for the Court, Chief Justice Burger focuses on the authority of the IRS to interpret the Internal Revenue Code in this case. He reasons as follows: The Internal Revenue code provides that "corporations . . . organized and operated exclusively for religious, charitable . . . or educational purposes are entitled to tax exemption." The "charitable" concept must conform to that common-law standard of charity, which requires an institution seeking tax exemption to serve "a public purpose and not be contrary to established public policy." Racial discrimination in education has been condemned by Supreme Court rulings, by the Congress in such enactments as the Civil Rights Act of 1964 and the Emergency School Act of 1978, and by Executive Orders, such as those of Eisenhower and Kennedy.

The following quotation summarizes the first line of argument and prepares us for the second: Few social or political issues in our history have been more

> vigorously debated and more extensively ventilated than the issue of racial discrimination, particularly in education. Given the stress and anguish of the history of efforts to escape from the shackles of the "separate but equal" doctrine of *Plessy v. Ferguson,* it cannot be said that educational institutions that, for whatever reasons, practice racial discrimination, are institutions exercising "beneficial and stabilizing influences in community life," or should be encouraged by having all taxpayers share in their support by way of special tax status.

Did the IRS overstep its lawful authority by revoking the tax exemption of the institutions based on its interpretation of the Internal Revenue Code? Isn't it the province of the Congress to alter the law to conform to public policy?

The reply of the Chief Justice is that Congress has expressly authorized the IRS commissioner to make the required rules and regulations for the enforcement of the tax laws. It is too much to expect the Congress to attend to the day-to-day oversight of so complex an operation. The interpretation by the IRS is consistent with established public policy that "discrimination on account of race is inconsistent with an *educational institution's* tax exempt status."

Doesn't this policy of the IRS interfere with the free exercise of sincerely held religious beliefs of those who have established Bob Jones University and the Goldsboro Christian Schools? The majority replies as follows:

> The governmental interest at stake here is compelling. . . . The Government has a fundamental, overriding interest in eradicating racial discrimination in education—discrimination that prevailed with official approval for the first 165 years of this Nation's history. That governmental interest substantially outweighs whatever burden denial of tax benefits places on petitioners' exercise of their religious beliefs. The interests asserted by petitioners cannot be accommodated with that compelling

governmental interest, and no "less restrictive means" . . . are available to achieve the governmental interest.

As for the argument that the denial of tax exemption violates the Establishment Clause by preferring religions which do not discriminate racially over those that do, the Court offers two answers. The IRS policy is based on a "neutral, secular basis" and, therefore, does not violate the Establishment Clause. In addition, the IRS rule applies to *all religiously operated schools,* thereby negating the need to inquire whether racial discrimination is the result of sincere religious belief.

Although Justice Powell joined in the opinion of the Court, he warned that the "contours of public policy should be determined by Congress, not by judges or the IRS." He was simply unwilling to accept the majority's dictum that the IRS had the authority to decide which public policies are so fundamental as to deny tax exemption.

Justice Rehnquist's dissent held that the IRS had no authority to decide on its own that private schools practicing racial discrimination are not entitled to tax-exempt status. This is the central responsibility of Congress, and the Court, he concluded, should not legislate for Congress. The schools in the case fit into the category of "educational institutions" as defined by the Internal Revenue Code, and they are entitled to tax exemption.

Pending Parochiaid Cases

Two potentially important opportunities to rewrite the constitutional principles of recent years are before the Court. *Grand Rapids School District v. Ball* poses the constitutionality of sending public school teachers into parochial school buildings to teach parochial school students. The courses ranged from remedial instruction to music and physical education. In Grand Rapids, public expenditures for this program rose from modest beginnings to $3 million in 1981-82, involved 11,000 parochial students, and included payment of rent to the parochial schools for use of their rooms. The program was enjoined and the case is pending before the High Court.

The second pending case, *Aguilar v. Felton,* involves the constitutionality of a New York policy which permits local school boards to send public school teachers into private schools to offer remedial math, reading, and English instruction to assist low-income, underachieving students. The money for this program comes out of Title I of the Elementary and Secondary Education Act of 1965.

In both cases, parochial school classrooms which were used for publicly funded courses had to be designated as public school classrooms and all religious symbols had to be removed or draped. [Editor's note: In 1985 the Supreme Court held both cases to be violative of the First Amendment.]

Equal Access for College Students?

There apparently is no limit to the variations possible under the religion clauses. In *Widmar v. Vincent,* 102 S. Ct. 269 (1981), we enter the thicket of equal access.

The University of Kansas provided facilities for meetings of officially registered student organizations. Under this policy, Cornerstone, an organization of evangelical Christian students, met from 1973-1977, when it was informed that it could no longer meet in the university buildings. The reason given was that Cornerstone meetings violated a 1972 university regulation prohibiting the use of its buildings "for purposes of religious worship or religious teaching."

Although twenty students formed the core of the club, its meetings were open to the public and attracted up to 125 students. These meetings included prayers, hymns, Bible commentary, and discussions of religious views and experiences.

The Cornerstone students invoked the First and Fourteenth Amendments against the university's change in policy. They appealed to free exercise of religion, freedom of speech, and equal protection under the law.

The university responded by arguing that its action was dictated by the Establishment Clause of the First Amendment, made applicable to the states by the Fourteenth Amendment, and by provisions of the Missouri Constitution, which required stricter separation of church and state than the provisions of the federal Constitution.

With only Justice White dissenting, the Court supported the position of the students. Justice Powell's opinion for the Court emphasizes that the university created a quasi-public forum by opening its buildings to registered student organizations. In such a forum and university atmosphere devoted to education, students have the right to freedom of speech and association. In this case, remarks the Justice, the university "has discriminated against student groups and speakers based on their desire to use a generally open forum to engage in religious worship and discussion." These are forms of speech and association protected by the First Amendment.

What we have here, points out the opinion, is the exclusion of a student group from this forum because of the religious content of its expression. The only justification for this is "a compelling state interest." Missouri argued that the compelling state interest is the separation of church and state mandated by the First Amendment and the Missouri Constitution.

However, says Justice Powell, when measured by the *Lemon* three-part rule, the university's open-forum regulation meets all three tests. Its purpose is secular because it provides a forum for religious and nonreligious speech; there is no excessive entanglement between government and religion; and the benefits that Cornerstone would receive from this forum, which is open to all forms of discourse, would be incidental. In other words, the primary purpose of the university regulation is not to advance religion. The university student handbook disclaims any approval by the university of views of the student organizations meeting there. Furthermore, in this case we are dealing with young college adults, not impressionable secondary school students. The college students should be able to understand that the university's policy is one of neutrality to religion. In addition, the Cornerstone meetings are open to religious and nonreligious students.

Therefore, continues the Justice, the university's invocation of the Establishment Clause is blunted by the Free Exercise of Religion and the Free Speech clauses of the amendment. He can find no compelling state interest in discriminating against the students on the basis of the religious content of their speech. An equal access policy, he concludes, is not incompatible with the Establishment Clause, if the policy meets the *Lemon* criteria.

The concluding paragraph of the opinion declares:

> The basis for our decision is narrow. Having created a forum generally open to student groups, the University seeks to enforce a content-based exclusion of *religious speech.* Its exclusionary policy violates the fundamental principle that a state regulation of speech should be content-neutral, and the University is unable to justify this violation under applicable constitutional standards.

In his concurring opinion, Justice Stevens agrees with the judgment of the Court, but finds that the reasoning unduly interferes with the right of the university to allocate its scarce resources as it sees fit. For example, the Court's use of such terms as "public forum" and "compelling state interest" complicate the case needlessly. He then resorts to examples that one does not ordinarily find in judicial rulings. The following quote illustrates this.

> Because every university's resources are limited, an educational institution must routinely make decisions concerning

the use of the time and space that is available for extracurricular activities. In my judgment, it is both necessary and appropriate for those decisions to evaluate the content of a proposed student activity. I should think it obvious, for example, that if two groups of 25 students requested the use of a room at a particular time — one to view Mickey Mouse cartoons and the other to rehearse an amateur performance of Hamlet — the First Amendment would not require that the room be reserved for the group that submitted its application first. Nor do I see why a university should have to establish a "compelling state interest" to defend its decision to permit one group to use the facility and not the other. In my opinion, a university should be allowed to decide for itself whether a program that illuminates the genius of Walt Disney should be given precedence over one that may duplicate material adequately covered in the classroom. Judgments of this kind should be made by academicians, not by federal judges, and their standards for decision should not be encumbered with ambiguous phrases like "compelling state interest."

In this case, however, the university's refusal to allow the Cornerstone students to engage in religious worship on the campus cannot be justified constitutionally. Since the activity was voluntary and, since the university had dissociated itself from sponsoring any particular religion, the university's fear of violating the Establishment Clause is "groundless."

For Justice White, the sole dissenter, the red flag is "religious speech." There is a world of difference, he points out, between religious speech and religious worship. The fact that religious worship uses speech does not bring it within the umbrella of First Amendment protections. Surely, there is a difference between religious services and worship, on the one hand, and talk about religious beliefs and religion, on the other, and a line must be drawn between them.

The university applied its regulation to Cornerstone only after it was informed by the students that they planned to offer prayers, singing of hymns, reading scripture, and teaching Biblical principles. Cornerstone students conceded that religious worship was an important part of their activities.

Has the state, through the university, imposed an unacceptable burden on the students' opportunity to practice their religious beliefs by denying them access to university facilities? By their own admission, the students indicated that, since they would now have to meet one and a half blocks from campus, they would be less comfortable and more inconvenienced. This burden, indicates the Justice, is so minimal as to be inconsequential.

Equal Access for High School Students? It Ain't Necessarily So

The case of *Widmar v. Vincent* does not end the story of equal access; it simply raises the curtain on the drama in the secondary schools. In *Widmar*, the Court remarked that college students are sufficiently mature to understand that equal access does not reflect a university's approval of religious speech or religious worship. Did that mean that the *Widmar* rule did not apply to secondary school students? The test was not long in coming.

As a matter of fact, the test actually began before *Widmar*. *Brandon v. Board of Education*, 635 F 2nd 971 (1980), dealt with the same type of issues. In September 1978, a group of high school students, calling themselves "Students for Voluntary Prayer," asked their principal for permission to conduct prayers at their high school before the official start of the school day. The principal of Guiderland High School, the superintendent of schools, and the board of education denied their request. The reason given was the Establishment Clause, which sets up a wall of separation between church and state. To grant the request, the authorities said, would be to violate the Constitution of the United States.

As is becoming customary in these types of cases, the students resorted to litigation. They argued that their case involved the Free Exercise of Religion, the Free Speech, and the Freedom of Association clauses of the First Amendment. To add greater weight to their balance in the scales of justice, they threw in the Equal Protection of the Laws Clause of the Fourteenth Amendment. All that they wanted, declared the students, was the right to engage in a voluntary student activity, to which other students were entitled, without benefit of faculty sponsorship or faculty advisors.

A United States district court dismissed the complaint of the students, and that ruling was affirmed by a United States court of appeals in 1980. The ruling pointed out that the public schools cannot be compared to a public forum, or a park, or a street corner where religious groups can air their views. A public school is a special institution of the state, and the state is required under the First and Fourteenth Amendments to respect the wall which separates the church from the state. The students are free to exercise their religion, but not in the school setting which they request. Since access to voluntary school prayer was denied to all religious groups, there is no merit to the claim of discrimination.

Since the Supreme Court refused to hear the appeal, the ruling of the court of appeals was sustained. However, other cases confront directly the issue as to whether public school officials can ban meetings by religious clubs in public secondary schools.

In *Bender v. Williamsport School District,* school authorities banned such meetings, and the response was as anticipated. In June 1982, several students and their parents sued on the grounds of free speech, right of association, free exercise of religion, and equal protection under law. They took no chances. Unimpressed, the school authorities informed them that the school rule was necessitated by judicial decisions prohibiting religious activities in public schools.

The students won in the federal district court. School authorities appealed and were supported by the Court of Appeals in the First Circuit, 741 F. 2d 538, (1984), which ruled that the *Widmar* case did not apply to high school students because they are at an impressionable age and because clubs in school buildings require faculty supervision. Since this will lead inevitably to excessive entanglement between church and state, the Widmar rule does not apply. Free speech in this type of case will have to give way to the Establishment Clause.

The Supreme Court has agreed to hear the case, and the Reagan Administration has filed an "amicus" brief on behalf of the students. The Bender ruling by the court of appeals was handed down in July 1984, shortly after Congress passed an equal access bill which requires public schools to provide all student organizations or student-initiated groups with equal access to school facilities. The bill was signed into law in August 1984.

Since the Bender case did not involve the equal access law, both the students in the case and the Reagan Administration felt that an adverse ruling might weaken the law. It is for this reason that the Administration intervened. [Editor's note: The Supreme Court chose not to render a definitive decision in *Bender,* but sent the case back to the district court for adjudication.]

Another case, in Lubbock, Texas emerged gradually as an equal access case. For a number of years during the 1970s, the Lubbock School District permitted teachers to lead students in classroom prayers and Bible reading over the school public address system. Bibles were distributed to elementary school children. When challenged in the courts, school officials promised to change this policy. When the case came before the United States Court of Appeals for the Fifth Circuit eight years later, it was found that the practice had not been stopped. In order to avoid the continuing controversy in this case, school board officials adopted a policy permitting student groups to use school facilities for meeting "so long as attendance at such meetings is voluntary," *Lubbock Independent School District v. Lubbock ACLU,* 669 F.2d 1038, (1982).

The federal court of appeals declared this policy unconstitutional under the Establishment Clause and prohibited the use of public school facilities for meetings of student religious groups before and after school hours.

The case was appealed to the Supreme Court, and twenty-four Senators filed an "amicus" brief urging the Court to support the Lubbock School district policy. Implicit in this intervention was the threat of the Senators' supporting a constitutional amendment to overrule a decision regarded as unsatisfactory.

Apparently unimpressed, in 1983 the High Court refused to take the case, thereby permitting the court of appeals ruling to be the final word — for the time being.

Churches, Schools, and Liquor Establishments

Grendel's Den, a restaurant in Cambridge, Massachusetts, applied for a liquor license. The Holy Cross Armenian Catholic Parish objected under a Massachusetts statute which empowered churches and schools to oppose such licenses to establishments located within a 500-foot radius of schools and churches. Would you regard this as another Establishment Clause case?

Eight Justices did and one did not. Chief Justice Burger, speaking for the majority in *Larkin v. Grendel's Den, Inc.*, 103 S. Ct. 505 (1982), concluded that the statute had delegated to schools (secular institutions) and to churches (religious institutions) a veto power over the granting of liquor licenses. This grant of zoning power to a church implicates the Establishment Clause. The fact that schools are included does not create a secular purpose. Since the church's power here is "standardless," and since there is no guarantee that the churches will not favor "liquor licenses for members of their congregations," the statute has the primary effect of advancing religion. In addition, this type of legislative veto in the hands of religious institutions tends to fuse governmental and religious functions, inviting excessive entanglement between church and state.

Justice Rehnquist's annoyance with the majority shows itself in his first paragraph. "Hard cases" and "great cases" make "bad law," but so do "silly cases," such as this one. What the majority has done, he complains, is transform "a quite sensible Massachusetts zoning law" into "some sort of sinister religious attack on secular government reminiscent of St. Bartholomew's Night."

The original statute, he points out, was a flat ban on alcoholic beverage licenses to any establishment within 500 feet of a church or school. What the legislature decided to do was to make the law more flexible by amending it to give churches or schools the opportunity to object. This type of legislative refinement and elimination of elaborate administrative agency hearings ought to be encouraged, rather than struck

71

down. It is unnecessary, he concludes, to use "heavy First Amendment artillery" to shoot down a sensible statute which in no way transforms churches into "third houses of the Massachusetts legislature."

Moments of Silence

At this time (Mid-April, 1985), the Wall Watchers are awaiting the judicial thunderclap in the Alabama moment of silence case. More than twenty states have passed a variety of statutes mandating voluntary prayers or moments of silence at the start of the school day. Some of the legislation focuses on silent meditation or reflection; others offer the option of prayer or meditation; and one even includes a disclaimer that "the moment of silent meditation shall not be intended or identified as a religious exercise."

In *Engel v. Vitale*, 82 S. Ct. 1261 (1962), the Court ruled 6 to 1 that the New York State Board of Regents had no business writing prayers for public school children. The following year an 8 to 1 decision in *Abington v. Schempp*, 83 S. Ct. 1560, outlawed required prayers and Bible reading in the public schools. Now the Court is about to answer the question of whether states can require students to engage in voluntary prayers or in moments of silence at the start of the school day.

The Alabama case before the Court, *Wallace v. Jaffree*, began with a lawsuit filed by an attorney who opposed the practice of prayers and grace before lunch initiated by teachers in the elementary schools attended by his children. The governor responded by calling the legislature into special session, and a law was passed permitting the use of a state-composed prayer at the start of class sessions (shades of *Engel v. Vitale*!). Jaffree included this prayer statute in his lawsuit and for good measure added another Alabama law, which apparently had never been implemented, permitting teachers to announce at the beginning of the first class of each school day a moment of silence or voluntary prayer. (This interesting story and the impact of these events on the life of Jaffree and his family is told in an article in the *ABA Journal,* April 1985, Vol. 71, pp. 61-64.)

Jaffree's lawsuit combined three causes of action: the constitutionality of the practice of teacher-led vocal prayers in the public schools, the governor's prayer law, and the moment of silence statute. Jaffree lost in the United States district court on all counts, but won in the court of appeals. Although the court granted a permanent injunction against vocal prayers, according to local observers the practice still continues in some schools. (One is compelled to wonder what kind of educators knowingly disobey a court injunction, while teaching their students to obey the law.) When the case came before the Supreme Court, the Justices summarily overturned the statute allowing public school teachers to lead students in spoken prayer. After all, this had been banned 22 years ago! At the same time, the Court agreed to review only the Alabama moment of silence law. Alabama had not appealed the permanent injunction which had originally led to the lawsuit.

Jaffree's lawyers argued before the Court that the statute violates the secular purpose and advancing religion parts of the *Lemon* trinity. Alabama pleaded for "modest accommodation" of the Establishment Clause to religious beliefs and practices.

Siding with Alabama, the Deputy Solicitor General of the United States took the position that the Alabama law was merely "informational" as to how the students can act during the silence.

Will the Court respond with a bang or a whimper? Will the Court, in view of the inflammatory nature of this controversy, engage in a hit-and-run tactic? That is, will it wait until the end of the present session, hand down its ruling on the last day, and run for cover? The losers in the case will not take their defeat lightly. [Editor's note: The Supreme Court struck down the Alabama law by a 6-3 vote in June, 1985. The Court concluded that Alabama authorities had impermissibly sought to promote religion through this law.]

Free Exercise of Religion

Up to this point, we have concentrated on the implications and ramifications of the first ten words of the First Amendment. We now turn to the next six words, which spell out freedom of religion.

In the Winter 1979 issue of *Update*, the article on religion explored the ripple effect of the Free Exercise of Religion Clause on the Mormons (polygamy), Amish (compulsory secondary education law), Jehovah's Witnesses (flag salute), and Seventh-day Adventists (Saturday sabbath).

We now examine briefly several recent cases. The first is *Heffron v. International Society for Krishna Consciousness (ISKCON)*, 101 S. Ct. 2559 (1981). The state agency operating the annual Minnesota state fair required all who distributed any merchandise, including printed or written materials, to do so only from a rented location on the fair grounds. The rule was designed, under the state's police power, to facilitate crowd control; to safeguard fairgoers from deceptive solicitations; and to protect them from annoyance and harassment. ISKCON protested that the rule was an unconstitutional infringement on their practice of Sankirtan — a religious ritual which requires them to go into public places to distribute religious literature and solicit donations.

The Court's decision was a 5 to 4 ruling. Justice White, speaking for the majority, declared that the state was justified in promulgating this rule, which served several important state interests, especially that of crowd control. Any state, he declared, has the power to impose reasonable time, place, and manner restrictions, provided they do not censor the content of speech. In addition, the rule in question is fair because it applies evenhandedly both to religious and nonreligious organizations and because the rentals are to be made on a first-come first-served basis.

The four dissenters agreed with the majority on the sale of materials and solicitation of funds, but felt that the Minnesota rule went too far with regard to distribution of literature. Speaking for Justices Stevens and Marshall, Justice Brennan dissented on the ground that the Minnesota rule should have been less restrictive, exempting the distribution of literature, a First Amendment right: "If fairgoers can make speeches, engage in face-to-face proselytizing, and buttonhole prospective supporters, they can surely distribute literature to members of their audience without significantly adding to the State's asserted crowd control problem." Justice Blackmun filed a separate dissent.

In view of these differences of opinion, it is difficult to assess how the Justices will react to airport and shopping malls issues.

Religious Beliefs and Unemployment Insurance

Let us suppose that a member of a religious sect quits his job rather than make turrets for military tanks. Can he get unemployment insurance?

This is exactly what happened to Thomas, a member of Jehovah's Witnesses, when he was working for a company in its roll foundry plant. When that plant was closed down, Thomas was transferred to the department which built turrets for military tanks. Opposed to war because of his religious beliefs, he refused to work in this department. Since all the work at the company now involved the production of military weapons, Thomas quit and applied for unemployment insurance.

The state refused to pay on the basis that Thomas did not have "good cause," as required by state law. The Supreme Court of Indiana agreed that Thomas had quit voluntarily for personal reasons and was, therefore, not entitled to benefits.

Had Thomas' right to exercise his religion under the First Amendment been violated by the state? Yes, said Chief Justice Burger, speaking for all of his brethren except Justice Rehnquist. In *Thomas v. Review Board of Indiana Employment Security Division,* 101 S. Ct. 1425 (1981), Burger concluded that Thomas had terminated his employment for religious reasons because he had been forced to make a choice between his religious belief and the loss of his job.

Did the state have a compelling reason to deny Thomas his benefits? It had argued that the "good cause" condition for unemployment insurance was enacted to prevent widespread unemployment for personal reasons and to avoid probing by employers into the religious beliefs of job applicants. Although these reasons are acceptable, says the Chief Justice, they do not justify in any way interference with or imposing burdens on the religious beliefs of workers.

However, if the state is required to pay benefits to Thomas, isn't it by implication advancing his religious faith and violating the Establishment Clause? Not so, says the Chief Justice, because in this case the government is assuming the stance of neutrality in the presence of religious differences. It is not singling out any religion and advancing it.

Justice Rehnquist begins his dissent with the charge that the majority "adds mud to the already muddied waters of the First Amendment." If, he says, there is tension between the Establishment Clause and the Free Exercise Clause, it is the "Court's own making." If the majority had applied the *Lemon* criteria, he points out, they would have concluded that the Indiana unemployment law conformed to all three guidelines. In essence, what we have here, he concludes, is a High Court ruling which requires a state "to provide direct financial assistance to persons solely on the basis of their religious beliefs."

No Photo, No Driver's License

Free exercise of religion cases do not reach the courts as often as do Establishment Clause cases, perhaps because the free exercise cases deal with very small idiosyncratic sects, while the establishment cases generally involve powerful religious organizations with considerable resources. As in Establishment Clause cases, the Court is constantly seeking to formulate a principle or rule of law which will help it resolve dilemmas of individual conscience and state power. Such a case is *Holly Jensen v. Frances J. Quaring,* argued on January 7, 1985, and not decided as of the time this article was written.

Frances Quaring had been driving for twenty years when the state of Nebraska denied her a driver's license because she refused to have her picture taken, as required by law. She explained that she believed in the literal interpretation of the Second Commandment: "Thou shall not make unto thee any graven images . . ." the issue was joined, and Quaring won in the federal district and appeals courts.

Before the Supreme Court, the state took the position that the right to drive is a privilege and not a right. It also based its case on the police powers of the state — the power to assist police officers with necessary identification; the power to stop the sale of alcoholic beverages to minors who drive; and the power to facilitate identification in financial transactions. In addition, the argument was made that to grant an exception in this case is to violate the Establishment Clause by aiding religion.

Quaring's response was that the photo requirement was a serious burden on her right to follow her religious beliefs. The state, she argued, can achieve identification by other means without interfering with religious beliefs. Finally, driving a car has become a necessity, and in certain areas it is the only mode of mobility. This development raises drivers' licenses to the level of a constitutional right which cannot be denied unless the state has a compelling reason, and, in this case, the state's position is untenable.

The Solicitor General of the United States intervened on behalf of Nebraska because, in part, the government is concerned about the growing refusal of some religious groups to use Social Security numbers. [Editor's note: By a 4-4 tie vote the Court affirmed the lower federal panel's ruling that Frances J. Quaring must be given her license.]

Conclusion

Despite the length of this article, it is not possible to do justice to all the important rulings of the last six years. For example, a 5 to 4 Court held in 1979 that the National Labor Relations Board had no jurisdiction over unions of lay teachers in church-operated secondary schools *(NLRB v. Catholic Bishops of Chicago,* 99 S. Ct. 1313). And pending before the Court now is the constitutionality of a Connecticut statute requiring private employers to give religious employees whatever day off they designate as a Sabbath. And then there are all those interesting decisions in the lower courts.

What is the condition of The Wall in mid-1985? It is not as high and impregnable as the Separatists want it to be, nor is it as low and vulnerable as the Accommodationists would like to see it. The Wall is still there and for some it continues to be a wailing wall, while for others it is a hailing wall. Built into the soil of history, it continues to stand as a reminder of our past and as a guide for our future.

The coming bicentennials of the drafting of the Constitution of the United States in 1987 and the ratification of the Bill of Rights in 1991 offer one of those rare historical opportunities to take inventory of where we have been as a nation, where we are, and where we should be heading. An important component of these national celebrations should be school-centered and community-wide dialogues, discourses, and discussions on the history, the philosophy, and the jurisprudence of the religion clauses as they have influenced our thinking about our unity and our diversity.

PART II   RESOURCES

The resources reviewed in the following pages are suitable for teaching about religious freedom in secondary schools. After an extensive search for the best available materials, these have been selected for their quality and balance. In some topic areas, unfortunately, there are far too few resources from which to choose. Nevertheless, there are enough audio-visual and printed classroom materials for an adequate presentation of religious liberty in U.S. history, government and law-related courses.

Materials have been divided into three topic areas in order to make it easier to select the supplementary resources appropriate for the time period and subject under consideration. Chapter 3 lists audio-visual and printed items for teaching about the origins of religious freedom in early America. Chapter 4 focuses on our religious diversity and on the conflicts and intolerance that have sometimes marred our history. Finally, Chapter 5 reviews materials concerning church-state court cases of the twentieth century that have shaped contemporary understanding of the religion clauses of the First Amendment.

We hope that teachers will use these materials and will encourage schools to purchase some of the more significant items. The addresses and phone numbers of all the distributors referred to in the text are listed in Appendix A. We suggest, of course, that teachers preview materials, particularly audio-visuals, before purchase.

3. FROM SALEM TO THE BILL OF RIGHTS

"Proclaim Liberty throughout all the land
unto all the inhabitants thereof."
Leviticus XXV, 10.

Inscription on the Liberty Bell

CLASSROOM MATERIALS

Audio-Visual

ANNE HUTCHINSON. Zenger Films, 1964. 50 minutes, videocassette.

Part of the award-winning television series "Profiles in Courage," this film dramatizes Anne Hutchinson's conflict with the Puritan Church in Massachusetts Bay Colony. Hutchinson is portrayed as a courageous and strong woman engaged in a serious religious dispute with the colony's leaders. Her dissension challenged the authority of the established church and led to her excommunication and banishment. The dilemma of the authorities, hard-pressed to carve out a new community under difficult circumstances, is also presented. Freedom of conscience is the central theme of the film. Theological issues are mentioned but not fully explained.

Available for purchase from Social Studies School Service.

IN SEARCH OF TOLERANCE. Granada Television International Ltd., 1978. 38 minutes, 16mm sound, color.

This is the best film available on the European background of the religious groups whose search for religious freedom brought them to America. An accurate and clear presentation of the persecution suffered by the Anabaptists, Huguenots, Puritans, and Quakers in Europe is followed by a useful overview of their struggles to settle in the New World. The film discusses the origins of the American concept of religious freedom and underscores the significance of early American religious developments that played a major role in shaping the new nation.

Available for rental or purchase from McGraw-Hill.

THE PURITAN EXPERIENCE: FORSAKING ENGLAND. Learning Corporation of America, 1975. 28 minutes, 16mm sound, color.

A well-written and nicely photographed dramatization of the conflicts between the Puritan reformers and the Church of England. Through the experience of the Higgins family, the film shows how the harassment of the established church drove thousands of Puritans to migrate to America in the 1630s.

Available for rental or purchase, 16mm or video, from Coronet/ MTI.

THE PURITAN EXPERIENCE: MAKING A NEW WORLD. Learning Corporation of America, 1975. 31 minutes, 16mm sound, color.

A continuation of the Higgins' story as they join the struggle to create a new community in Massachusetts based on Puritan ideals. The young girl in the family befriends the Indians and objects to their cruel treatment by the Puritans. Her unorthodox behavior and beliefs eventually force her family to leave the colony. In places the film presents a simplistic and frightening picture of the Puritan faith in contrast to an overly romantic view of Indian practices. Despite this weakness, the story does raise important issues about freedom of conscience and religion.

Available for rental or purchase, 16mm or video, from Coronet/ MTI.

RELIGIOUS FREEDOM IN AMERICA'S BEGINNINGS. Coronet Films, 1971. 14 minutes, 16mm sound, color.

A concise and thoughtful overview of the genesis of religious freedom in colonial America. The film makes the important point that religious toleration was thrust upon the young nation by a variety of economic, political, and philosophical circumstances.

Available for rental or purchase from Coronet/MTI.

ROGER WILLIAMS: FOUNDER OF RHODE ISLAND. Encyclopaedia Britannica Films, 1956. 28 minutes, 16mm sound, black and white.

An adequate, if a bit sentimental, portrait of Roger Williams, one of the key figures in the evolution of religious freedom in America. The film describes how Williams' theological concern for the purity of the church leads him to oppose state involvement in matters of faith. Tried and banished for his views, Williams establishes a new colony and promotes freedom of religion. A good film for use in a discussion about the origins of church-state separation in America.

Available for rental or purchase from Encyclopaedia Britannica Educational Corporation.

WALL OF SEPARATION.   Bauman Bible Telecasts, 1975. 28 minutes, 16mm sound, color.

This film explores the origins of the principle of church-state separation in America. After a brief historical perspective on church and state issues in the Colonial period, there is an excellent summary of how our Founding Fathers understood the "wall of separation." The views of Jefferson, Madison, Franklin, Hamilton and others are represented in the balanced and clear narrative.

Available for rental from Bauman Bible Telecasts.

WEST TO FREEDOM.   Anti-Defamation League. 21 minutes, filmstrip, cassette, color.

The story of the many religious and ethnic groups in early America and the important role they played in the struggle for independence. Jews, Blacks, Poles, Catholics and others barely mentioned in most textbooks are portrayed here as having made significant contributions to the Revolution. Religious diversity and the demand for religious freedom are strong themes of the filmstrip.

Available for purchase from the Anti-Defamation League.

WILLIAM PENN AND THE QUAKERS.   Coronet Films. 15 minutes, 16mm sound, color.

A documentary about the founding of Pennsylvania by William Penn. Though the persecution of Quakers in England is noted, little is said about Quaker beliefs or practices. Penn's ideals, including religious freedom, are treated very briefly.

Available for rental or purchase, 16mm or video, from Coronet/MTI.

THE WITCHES OF SALEM: THE HORROR AND THE HOPE. Learning Corporation of American, 1972. 34 minutes, 16mm sound, color.

Using dialogue based on actual court testimony, this film recreates the events surrounding the Salem witchcraft trials of 1692. Though the religious beliefs of the Puritans are inadequately explored, the film remains an interesting portrayal of a theocratic society in which the intolerance of nonconformity contributes to the persecution of innocent people.

Available for rental or purchase, 16mm or video, from Coronet/ MTI.

Printed

THE CONSTITUTION: EVOLUTION OF A GOVERNMENT. Social Issues Resources Series, Inc. and the National Archives, 1985.

This teaching unit reproduces thirty-four documents from the National Archives carefully chosen to supplement the study of the constitutional period and constitutional issues. Part III, "The Evolution of a Constitutional Issue," does an excellent job of introducing students to the complexities of the religion clauses of the First Amendment. Other sections discuss how the Constitution came to be and consider some of the challenges facing the new government. The teacher's guide provides classroom exercises designed for various ability levels as well as worksheets and an annotated bibliography. This unit, like the previous National Archives/SIRS publications, encourages critical thinking about significant issues in American history.

Available for purchase from Social Issues Resources Series, Inc.

FREEDOM AND AUTHORITY IN PURITAN NEW ENGLAND. Allen Guttmann. Addison-Wesley Publishing Co., 1970.

Part of the Amherst Project series, this fifty-page unit focuses on two conflicts in Puritan New England. The first concerns the dispute between Thomas Morton of Merry-Mount and the Pilgrim Fathers who objected to what they saw as Morton's "pagan" behavior. The second part of the unit considers the controversy surrounding Roger Williams' objections to the theocracy of Massachusetts Bay Colony. In both cases, the story is presented first as seen by the original participants, and then by historians of succeeding generations. This arrangement reveals to the student how the same events may be viewed quite differently depending on the perspective and time period of the observer. A thought-provoking introduction to Puritan theocracy.

Although out of print, a limited number of back copies are available from Addison-Wesley Publishing Co.

TWO HUNDRED YEARS OF MR. JEFFERSON'S IDEA: THE EXPANSION OF RELIGIOUS FREEDOMS IN THE UNITED STATES. Melvin I. Urofsky and Philip E. Urofsky. Virginia Department of Education, 1986.

Written for teachers and students, this booklet is a good overview of the story of religious freedom in America. The authors trace the evolution in U.S. history of the ideas embodied in Jefferson's famous Statute For Religious Freedom, adopted in Virginia in 1786. The appendix includes twenty-three documents concerning religious liberty issues from various periods in our history.

Available from the Virginia Department of Education.

Suggestions For Background Reading

Alley, Robert S., ed. *James Madison on Religious Liberty.* Buffalo: Prometheus Books, 1985.

This excellent book is the first publication in one volume of James Madison's writings on religious freedom. Also included are essays by scholars and statesmen on the religion clauses of the First Amendment and the legacy of Madison. For teachers and students.

Antieau, Chester James, Arthur T. Downey, and Edward C. Roberts. *Freedom From Federal Establishment: Formation and Early History of the First Amendment Religion Clauses.* Milwaukee: The Bruce Publishing Co., 1963.

A good, scholarly history covering church-state relations in colonial America and the origins of the First Amendment. For teachers and advanced students.

Bremer, Francis J., ed. *Anne Hutchinson: Troubler of the Puritan Zion.* Huntington, N.Y.: Robert E. Krieger Publishing Co., 1981.

A collection of scholarly articles by historians on the conflict between Anne Hutchinson and the Puritan Commonwealth. Very helpful for understanding the personality and religious views of this remarkable woman. For teachers and advanced students.

Carroll, Peter N., ed. *Religion and the Coming of the American Revolution.* Waltham, Mass.: Grim and Co., 1970.

Sermons and writings of Jonathan Edwards, Charles Chauncey and others documenting the religious background of the split between Great Britain and the American colonies. Valuable for understanding the theological and moral arguments used to justify the Revolution. For teachers and advanced students.

Curry, Thomas J. *The First Freedoms: Church and State in America to the*

Passage of the First Amendment. New York: Oxford University Press, 1986.

A splendid new study of church and state in colonial and revolutionary America. This is the best and most comprehensive book available on the historical origins and background of the religion clauses of the First Amendment. Highly recommended for teachers and students.

Cousins, Norman, ed. *In God We Trust: The Religious Beliefs and Ideas of the American Founding Fathers.* New York: Harper and Brothers, 1958.

A useful, clear presentation of the religion of the men who founded the nation. Important background reading for teachers and students.

Dunn, Mary M. *William Penn: Politics and Conscience.* Princeton: Princeton University Press, 1967.

A highly readable account of Penn's political activities, particularly his struggle to promote freedom of conscience. One of the most complete and balanced discussions of Penn's thinking available. For teachers and students.

Hanley, Thomas O'Brien. *Their Rights and Liberties: The Catholic Tradition of Freedom in Maryland.* Chicago: Loyola University Press, 1984.

A good account of colonial Maryland's experiment in religious toleration under the Ordinance of 1639, an important early chapter in the story of religious freedom in America. For teachers and students.

Healey, Robert M. *Jefferson on Religion in Public Education.* New Haven: Yale University Press, 1962.

A scholarly exploration of Jefferson's philosophy concerning the relationship of religion, the principle of church-state separation, and public education. The author connects Jefferson's views to present-day debates about the role of religion in the schools. For teachers.

Miller, Glenn T. *Religious Liberty in America: History and Prospects.* Philadelphia: The Westminster Press, 1976.

A concise and readable history of religious freedom in America. Unfortunately, readers will have to rely on library copies as this book is out of print. Particularly recommended for students.

Miller, Perry. *Roger Williams: His Contribution to the American Tradition.* Indianapolis: Bobbs-Merrill Co., 1953.

This collection of Roger Williams' writings brings to life one of the best known but least understood figures of American history. Miller's careful editing and excellent commentary make this book essential reading for learning about this great proponent of religious freedom. For teachers and students.

Miller, Perry and Thomas H. Johnson. *The Puritans.* New York, The American Book Co., 1938.

A rich collection of Puritan writings that allows the Puritans to speak for themselves. Good background for understanding Puritan theocracy and the Roger Williams, Anne Hutchinson controversies.

Morgan, Edmund S. *Roger Williams: The Church and State.* New York: Harcourt Brace & World Inc., 1967.

A lucid examination of the evolution of Williams' thinking about the church, the state and the relationship between them. Recommended for teachers and advanced students interested in the theological roots of Williams' commitment to religious freedom.

Smith, Elwyn A. *Religious Liberty in the United States.* Philadelphia: Fortress Press, 1972.

A detailed look at the evolution of church-state thought in America. Smith identifies and analyzes three basic categories of thought: the separatist, the Catholic, and the constitutional. For teachers.

Winslow, Ola. *Master Roger Williams.* New York: Macmillan, 1957.

A thorough, scholarly biography of Rhode Island's founder. For teachers and students.

4. MINORITY FAITHS AND MAJORITY RULE

"May the children of the Stock of Abraham, who dwell in this land, continue to merit and enjoy the good will of the other Inhabitants; while every one shall sit in safety under his own vine and figtree, and there shall be none to make him afraid. May the father of all mercies scatter light and not darkness in our paths, and make us all in our several vocations useful here, and in his own due time and way everlastingly happy."

— George Washington

From Washington's letter to the Hebrew Congregation in Newport, Rhode Island, August 17, 1790

CLASSROOM MATERIALS

Audio-Visual

ALEXANDER WILLIAM DONIPHAN. Zenger Films, 1964. 50 minutes, videocassette.

Based on the events surrounding the expulsion of the Mormons from Missouri in the 1830s, this film tells the story of Alexander Doniphan, a political leader and a general in the militia. Doniphan attempted to give fair treatment to the Mormons in a territory hostile to their presence. When violence erupted, the Mormon prophet Joseph Smith was captured and sentenced to die. Doniphan, believing Smith to have been unlawfully convicted, refused to carry out the order to execute him. By defending the unpopular Mormons and following the dictates of his conscience, Doniphan sacrificed a promising political career. Though generally a good production, the film unfortunately fails to engage the religious issues involved. The viewer is offered a one-dimensional, sentimental view of the Mormons with very little background concerning their beliefs and practices. The reasons for the tension between the Mormons and other groups are never made clear. If these gaps are filled in by the teacher, the film can be a valuable resource for discussing the importance of defending the rights of religious groups whose practices may cause discomfort to the majority in a given area of the country. Part of the "Profiles in Courage" series.

Available for purchase from Social Studies School Service.

THE AMISH: A PEOPLE OF PRESERVATION. Heritage Productions. 53 minutes, 16mm sound, color.

A sympathetic and comprehensive documentary about the Amish, a small, Christian sect famous for its adherence to a simple life in a complex modern world. Following a brief history of the Amish, the film gives a detailed picture of Amish daily life, including an interesting look at the attitudes of the younger members. A good background film for a discussion of the Free Exercise Clause of the First Amendment, particularly in light of the 1972 Supreme Court decision exempting Amish children beyond primary school age from the compulsory school attendance laws.

Available for rental or purchase from Encyclopaedia Britannica Educational Corp.

DESECRATION IN DARKNESS: A COMMUNITY FIGHTS BACK. Anti-Defamation League. 18 minutes, videocassette, color.

Recounts a recent incident in Silver Spring, Maryland, in which a synagogue was desecrated with Nazi symbols and hate slogans. Outraged by this ugly display of anti-Semitism, many people in the community from various faiths came forward to participate in the clean-up effort. Eight vandals were arrested and religious vandalism legislation was passed. While this story illustrates the tragic fact that anti-Semitism remains a problem in our country, it also reveals the willingness of a cross-section of the community to fight against intolerance and prejudice.

Available for purchase in video from the Anti-Defamation League.

FREE TO BE? Anti-Defamation League. 28 minutes, 16mm sound, color.

A thought-provoking look at the religious and ethnic diversity of American society. The point is made that freedom in our country has been won only after a long struggle beginning with the Puritan dissenters and continuing through our history with the efforts of women, Blacks and others to gain equality. Diversity brings with it tensions as each new wave of immigrants arrive with new customs and beliefs. Cultural pluralism, while enriching our society, has also spawned intolerance, exclusion and bigotry. The film asks the viewer to think about questions raised by diversity and conformity in American life. What are the values of group loyalty and identification, and what degree of assimilation is desirable in order to foster a united nation?

Available in 16mm for rental or purchase, or video for purchase only from the Anti-Defamation League.

JEWS IN AMERICA. Anti-Defamation League. Part I, "The Ingathering," 19 minutes. Part II, "Inside the Golden Door," 20 minutes. Filmstrip, cassette, color.

This two-part filmstrip tells the story of 300 years of Jewish life in America and in the process illuminates an often neglected dimension of U.S. history. From participation in the growth and development of the colonies to present-day involvement in American society, the filmstrip discusses how Jews have helped to shape our nation. A central theme of the story is the struggle against discrimination in the search for religious freedom and tolerance for Jews . . . and for all Americans. A discussion guide containing background information and annotated bibliography is included.

Available for purchase from the Anti-Defamation League.

JOHN M. SLATON. Zenger Films, 1964. 50 minutes, videocassette.

The 1913 trial of Leo Frank for murder stirred up intense anti-Semitism in Georgia, contributing to Frank's conviction and death sentence. This film relates how Governor Slaton came to doubt Frank's guilt. Fighting popular sentiment and risking his political future, Slaton commuted the death sentence to life imprisonment. This action did not, however, prevent Frank's lynching by a mob. Though very good, the film needs to be supplemented by a discussion of the anti-Semitism of the period, a topic not dealt with in the script. Part of the "Profiles in Courage" series.

Available for purchase from Social Studies School Service.

THE KU KLUX KLAN: AN AMERICAN PARADOX. New York Times, 1982. 20 minutes, filmstrip, color.

An examination of past and present activities of the KKK throughout the United States. The filmstrip does a good job of exploring the reasons for the Klan's recent resurgence. A helpful discussion guide is included.

Available for purchase from the Anti-Defamation League.

KU KLUX KLAN: THE INVISIBLE EMPIRE. CBS-TV. 45 minutes, 16mm sound, black and white.

This powerful CBS Reports documentary of the KKK contains the first filmed sequences of a Klan initiation ritual as well as vivid shots of a Klan rally and cross-burning. Interviews with Klan members lay bare the mindset that has led to violent acts against Blacks, Jews, Catholics and others throughout the history of the Klan.

Available in 16mm for rental or purchase, or in video for purchase only from the Anti-Defamation League.

THE LITTLE FALLS INCIDENT. WCBS-TV. 7 minutes, 16mm sound, color.

When an anti-Semitic incident occurred in the junior high school of a small New Jersey town, a reporter interviewed the people involved including a Jewish girl who was the victim, her classmates, her teacher, her mother and the school principal. Their reactions, recorded in this film, suggest that although anti-Semitism remains a problem in our society, many people refuse to confront it directly. Useful for initiating discussion about anti-Semitism and other forms of prejudice.

Available for rental or purchase from the Anti-Defamation League.

MARY McDOWELL. Zenger Films, 1964. 50 minutes, videocassette.

The true story of Mary McDowell, a Quaker teacher at a New York high school during World War I. In the midst of the nation's patriotic fervor, McDowell refused to sign a loyalty oath or take part in war support activities because of her faith. Her stand resulted in her dismissal. The moral dilemmas of pacifism are discussed briefly in the film, but little more is said about McDowell's Quaker beliefs. A good film for initiating discussion about the conflict some religious groups face between following their consciences and obedience to the law. It also raises questions about when and if the state has the right to limit free exercise of religion. Part of the "Profiles in Courage" series.

Available for purchase from Social Studies School Service.

THE MORMON EXPERIENCE: THE DESIRE TO BE DIFFERENT IN AMERICA. Multi-Media Productions. Two color filmstrips, cassette, guide.

The persecution suffered by the Mormons in the 19th century is a tragic chapter in the story of religious freedom in America. This two-part filmstrip describes Joseph Smith and the Mormon odyssey across the country in search of a place to freely practice their faith. There is a balanced discussion of how and why conflicts arose between the Mormons and their neighbors.

Available for purchase from Social Studies School Service.

RELIGIOUS DIVERSITY. Moctesuma Esparza Productions. 18 minutes, 16mm sound, color.

A colorful glimpse of religious life in the United States. The film suggests that religious freedom and tolerance allow many faiths to flourish in one nation. After a brief historical perspective, there are a few images of the practices of the major faiths in America: Christianity, Judaism, Islam, and Buddhism. Young people involved in these groups describe how they understand their faith. This film may be a useful way to get students talking about the importance of tolerance in a pluralistic society.

Available for purchase or rental from Phoenix Films.

RENDEZVOUS WITH FREEDOM. ABC-TV. 37 minutes, 16mm, color.

An edited version of the ABC documentary, this film tells the story of Jewish immigration to America from 1654 until the 20th century. Fleeing persecution in Europe, the Jews came seeking religious freedom. The film discusses how they have been able to create a new life in the New World, though even here freedom must be fought for and the problem of anti-Semitism persists.

Available for rental from the Anti-Defamation League.

WOODROW WILSON. Zenger Films, 1964. 50 minutes, videocassette.

The account of President Wilson's nomination of Louis Brandeis, the first Jew named to the Supreme Court. Wilson courageously defended his choice against strong political opposition and in the face of ugly anti-Semitism. Part of the "Profiles in Courage" series.

Available for purchase from Social Studies School Service.

Printed

EXTREMIST GROUPS IN THE UNITED STATES: A CURRICULUM GUIDE. Anti-Defamation League. 315 pages.

Throughout U.S. history extremist organizations of the left and right have threatened our basic freedoms, including freedom of religion. In this valuable book, teachers are given some of the materials needed to instruct students concerning the beliefs and tactics of extremist groups in America. The fourteen topics covered include in-depth examinations of the Ku Klux Klan, neo-Nazis and leftist terrorists. Each section has a series of readings for the student as well as an outline of classroom objectives and activities.

Available for purchase from the Anti-Defamation League.

JEWS IN AMERICAN HISTORY: A TEACHER'S GUIDE. Jerome Ruderman. Anti-Defamation League, 1974. 224 pages.

Jewish history in the United States has been neglected in the social studies curriculum of our secondary schools. This book is a good resource for helping to correct that deficiency. The eight chapters cover major periods of American history and disuss the roles Jews played in the development of our nation. The book makes clear that the story of American Jews is a significant dimension of the struggle for religious freedom. Each chapter includes discussion questions, student activities, and a bibliography of books and audio-visual materials.

Available for purchase from the Anti-Defamation League.

MINORITY RELIGIONS IN AMERICA. William J. Whalen. Alba House, 1981. 226 pages.

A balanced, readable survey of twenty-six faiths in the United States. Sections on the Jehovah's Witnesses, Mormons, Mennonites, and Quakers may be useful in the classroom as background information on key religious freedom conflicts.

Available for purchase from the Social Studies School Service.

Suggestions For Background Reading

Ahlstrom, Sydney E. *A Religious History of the American People.* New Haven: Yale University Press, 1972.

The best one-volume history of American religion available, this absorbing study reveals the significant role religion has played in American life from the days of the first settlers to the present. A superb reference for teachers and students.

Belth, Nathan C. *A Promise to Keep.* New York: Times Books, 1979.

A good account of anti-Semitism in America from the Colonial Period to the 1970s. Although the narrative focuses on Jewish efforts to secure religious freedom, the book succeeds in telling the larger story of America's battle with prejudice and intolerance. Recommended especially for students.

Blau, Joseph, ed. *Cornerstones of Religious Freedom in America*. Boston: Beacon Press, 1965.

A collection of basic documents on the subject of religious freedom. The choice of material reflects Blau's strong advocacy of strict church-state separation. A helpful reference for teachers and students.

Bromley, David G. and James T. Richardson, eds. *The Brainwashing/ Deprogramming Controversy: Sociological, Psychological, Legal and Historical Perspectives*. New York: Edwin Mellen Press, 1983.

Twenty articles on various dimensions of the First Amendment problems surrounding some of the new religious movements in America. For teachers.

Chalmers, David M. *Hooded Americanism: The First Century of the Ku Klux Klan, 1865-1965*. Garden City: Doubleday, 1965.

A detailed, authoritative history of the Ku Klux Klan from its founding in 1865 to recent events. For teachers and students.

Golden, Harry. *A Little Girl is Dead*. Cleveland: World Publishing Co., 1965.

A moving, dramatic retelling of the arrest, trial and lynching of Leo Frank in Georgia. For teachers and students.

Handy, Robert T. *A Christian America: Protestant Hopes and Historical Realities*. New York: Oxford University Press, 1971.

An excellent discussion of the Protestant vision of a Christian America. The author contends that many current church-state problems are rooted in an earlier "Protestant era" of American history. For teachers.

Hostetler, John A. *Amish Society*. Baltimore: Johns Hopkins Press, 1963.

A well-written study of the Amish by a scholar who was born and reared in an Amish community. A good exploration of the tensions between the Amish and governmental regulations that have raised a number of First Amendment questions. For teachers and students.

Lincoln, C. Eric. *The Black Muslims in America*. Boston: Beacon Press, 1973.

An objective study of the origins and significance of the Black Muslims, a movement that aroused considerable controversy. For teachers and students.

Marty, Martin E. *Righteous Empire: The Protestant Experience in America*. New York: Dial Press, 1970.

This is one of the best books available on the role and significance of Protestantism in American history. For teachers and advanced students.

Menendez, Albert J. *Religious Conflict in America: A Bibliography*. New York: Garland Publishing, Inc., 1985.

An extensive listing of books and articles dealing with religious conflict in U.S. history. Arranged chronologically, the entries reflect a wide range of political and religious perspectives. Useful for teachers and students.

Needelman, Jacob. *The New Religions*. New York: E. P. Dutton, 1977.

A balanced, readable account of some of the new religious movements in the United States. Unlike many writers on the subject, the author evidences a careful understanding of the beliefs and practices of the faiths discussed. Although a bit dated, this book remains a good introduction to these movements. For teachers and students.

Nelson, Hart M., Raytha Yokley, and Anne Nelsen, eds. *The Black Church in America*. New York: Basic Books, 1971.

A collection of writings by scholars and Black leaders on the Black church in America. Taken together, these writings provide valuable insights on the centrality of the church to the Black experience in this country. For teachers and advanced students.

Quinley, Harold E. and Charles Y. Glock. *Anti-Semitism in America*. New Brunswick, N.J.: Transaction Books, 1983.

A provocative study of prejudice in our society drawn from nationwide surveys on anti-Semitism. This carefully researched volume is an important reference for teachers and students.

Rosten, Leo, ed. *Religions of America: Ferment and Faith in an Age of Crisis*. New York: Touchstone, 1975.

A useful outline of the basic beliefs of the major religious groups in the United States. Also included are the views of each faith on controversial social issues such as abortion and homosexuality. The second part of the book is an almanac of polls and statistics covering a wide variety of questions confronting religion in contemporary society. A handy reference for teachers and students.

5. CHURCH, STATE, AND THE COURTS

"I contemplate with sovereign reverence that act of the whole American people which declared that their legislature should 'make no law respecting an establishment of religion or prohibiting the free exercise thereof,' thus building a wall of separation between church and state."
— Thomas Jefferson

From Jefferson's letter to the Danbury Baptist Association, January 1, 1802

CLASSROOM MATERIALS

Audio-Visual

THE BILL OF RIGHTS IN ACTION: FREEDOM OF RELIGION. B. Fass, 1969. 21 minutes, 16mm sound, color.

Focusing on a blood transfusion case, this film examines what happens if laws are broken or life is endangered through the free exercise of religion. After a car accident, a pregnant woman, supported by her husband, refuses on religious grounds a blood transfusion that would save her life and the life of her unborn child. In an emergency hearing, lawyers on both sides argue the constitutional issues before a judge. The viewer is asked to consider at what point the interest of society outweighs the individual's religious freedom. The Constitutional Rights Foundation has designed a lesson plan to accompany this film ("Do You Believe?" — reviewed below). These materials are an excellent way to initiate student discussion about the meaning of the Free Exercise Clause of the First Amendment.

Available for rental or purchase from Barr Films.

INHERIT THE WIND. United Artists. 127 minutes, videocassette, black and white.

A slightly fictionalized and highly dramatic reenactment of the Scopes trial starring Frederic March and Spencer Tracy as William Jennings Bryan and Clarence Darrow respectively.

Available for purchase from Social Studies School Service.

RELIGION AND POLITICS: TESTING OUR DEMOCRACY. Close Up Foundation, 1985. 60 minutes, videocassette, color.

The Reverend Robert Drinan, a Georgetown University Law

Center Professor, and the Reverend Jerry Falwell, founder of the Moral Majority, answer questions from students on a number of controversial church-state issues including textbook censorship, school prayer, and aid to parochial schools. The question and answer format does not, in this case, provoke much interaction between the two speakers, leaving the viewer unclear about just where they disagree. Unfortunately, the moderator fails to urge clarification of a number of vague answers by both men. Used selectively and with appropriate background to the issues, this exchange might be a useful stimulus for classroom discussion.

Available for rental or purchase from Close Up Foundation.

RELIGION AND PUBLIC SCHOOLS. Educational Enrichment Materials, 1982. 11 minutes, color filmstrip, cassette.

The debates concerning prayer in schools and the teaching of creationism are introduced here in clear and concise terms. The viewer is given both sides of the argument and then asked to form an opinion. Used in conjunction with appropriate background readings, this filmstrip can help focus classroom discussion about two difficult issues. The National Street Law Institute developed this and five additional programs on various aspects of the law which directly affect the lives of students.

Available for purchase from Random House.

THE SCHEMPP CASE: BIBLE READING IN PUBLIC SCHOOLS. Encyclopaedia Britannica in collaboration with Isidore Starr, 1969. 35 minutes, 16mm sound, color.

A well-written, balanced dramatization of the famous School District of Abington Township vs. Schempp case concerning Bible reading in public schools. The Abington Township schools broadcast Bible reading and prayer throughout their classrooms. The Schempp family objected, arguing that these practices were contrary to their beliefs and violated the First Amendment. The town contended that these programs were of moral and educational benefit and did not prefer one sect at the expense of others. The Supreme Court ruled in favor of the Schempps, holding that Bible reading and other religious exercises in public schools violate the Establishment Clause. The film is a very good presentation of a key church-state case and a useful way to introduce the complexities surrounding the meaning of the separation of church and state.

Available for rental or purchase from Encyclopaedia Britannica Corporation.

THE SCOPES TRIAL. Educational Enrichment Material, 1982. color filmstrip and cassette.

Part of the "Great American Trials" series, this filmstrip recreates the 1925 "monkey trial" of John Scopes who was under indictment for teaching evolution in Tennessee. In the famous courtroom battle between William Jennings Bryan and Clarence Darrow, Fundamentalist religious convictions collided with modern scientific theories. A good, brief introduction to the creationism vs. evolution debate that is still being argued today.

Available for purchase from Social Studies School Service.

Printed

THE CONSTITUTION: EVOLUTION OF A GOVERNMENT. Social Studies Resource Series, Inc. and the National Archives. 1985. (see annotation in Chapter 3)

DO YOU BELIEVE?: RELIGIOUS RIGHTS IN THE PUBLIC SCHOOLS. Estelle Howard and Richard Weintraub. Constitutional Rights Foundation. 1982.

A lesson plan covering such freedom of religion issues as school prayer and religious activity in public schools. One unit requires viewing the film The Bill of Rights in Action: Freedom of Religion (reviewed above), another involves the participation of a lawyer, and a third is a role-playing simulation of a school prayer case. These units offer a creative and thoughtful approach to difficult issues.

Available for purchase from the Constitutional Rights Foundation.

GOD AND GOVERNMENT: THE UNEASY SEPARATION OF CHURCH AND STATE. Allen Guttmann. Addison-Wesley Publishing Company. 1972. 49 pages.

This brief unit, developed as part of the Amherst Project, focuses primarily on two controversies that have confronted the American Roman Catholic Church: the relationship of traditional Church teachings to the American experiment of church-state separation, and the debate surrounding the question of federal aid to parochial schools.

Out of print, but a limited number of back copies are available for purchase from Addison-Wesley Publishing Company.

THE IDEA OF LIBERTY: FIRST AMENDMENT FREEDOMS. Isidore Starr. West Publishing Company. 1978. 234 pages.

In this excellent textbook, Isidore Starr succeeds admirably in bringing to life the meaning and significance of the First Amendment. The first two of six sections are devoted to a thoughtful consideration of the religion clauses. Starr draws on landmark Supreme Court cases to illustrate the evolution of the idea of religious freedom in American history. One of the many strengths of this text is its use of the case study method. Facts from key Court cases are presented and the student is asked to analyze the issues and to give an opinion before reading how the Court ruled.

Available for purchase from West Publishing Co.

LIVING WITH THE FIRST AMENDMENT IN THE 80's: CHALLENGES FOR CITIZENSHIP EDUCATION. Council for the Advancement of Citizenship. 1985.

A useful and balanced collection of recent articles from various periodicals on church-state relations in America. Contrasting historical perspectives are given by R. Freeman Butts and Senator Orrin Hatch. Many of the articles selected focus on three contemporary church-state issues of particular importance for schools: school prayer, creationism, and tuition tax credits. Also included is a provocative exchange of letters between President Reagan and Norman Lear debating the meaning of religious freedom.

Available for purchase from the Council for the Advancement of Citizenship.

RELIGION. Social Issues Resources Series (SIRS). Vols. 1 and 2.

These two loose-leaf volumes contain carefully selected articles on religion from a wide range of newspapers, magazines, government publications, and journals. This is a valuable resource for informing students about recent developments in religion, and for helping them to understand the religious dimension of many political and social questions in American society. SIRS publishes thirty-one other collections of articles on everything from defense to sports. Updated annually.

Available for purchase from Social Issues Resources Series, Inc.

RELIGION, MORALITY AND AMERICAN EDUCATION. BILL OF RIGHTS IN ACTION. Vol. XVII, No.1. February/March 1983.

Designed for classroom use, this 23-page magazine contains clear and informative discussions of key church-state debates concerning censorship, creationism, school prayer, and "secular humanism". In addition there is a helpful, if brief, summary of the history of religion in American schools. There are also activities for student discussion and writing.

A free subscription to the *Bill of Rights in Action* as well as other excellent materials for law-related education are available from the Constitutional Rights Foundation.

RELIGIOUS FREEDOM. Leo Pfeffer. National Textbook Company and the American Civil Liberties Union. 1977. 181 pages.

A comprehensive collection of documents, primarily Supreme Court opinions, tracing the development of the religion clauses in American history. Noted scholar Leo Pfeffer provides a clear and concise commentary. This is a valuable reference tool that might be useful as a text for advanced students.

Available for purchase from National Textbook Company.

UPDATE ON LAW RELATED EDUCATION. American Bar Association.

Update, an award-winning magazine published three times a year (fall, winter, and spring), is an indispensible resource for teachers and students interested in the latest developments in freedom of religion and other constitutional issues. Excellent articles by noted educators offer full coverage of trends in the law, including Supreme Court previews and decisions. (The articles by Isidore Starr in Chapter 2 of this guide are reprinted from *Update.*) Each issue also contains helpful classroom strategies and reviews of recent curriculum materials.

Subscriptions, back issues, and a special packet on the Constitution and Bill of Rights are available from the American Bar Association.

Suggestions For Background Reading

Butts, R. Freeman. *The American Tradition in Religion and Education.* Boston: Beacon Press, 1950.

A now classic study of the meaning of church-state separation for education in the U.S. Particularly valuable for its in-depth examination of the relationship of religion and education throughout our history. Recommended for teachers seeking an historical perspective on current debates about religion in the schools.

Ginger, Ray. *Six Days or Forever?: Tennessee v. John Thomas Scopes.* Boston: Beacon Press, 1958.

The most interesting account available of the famous "monkey trial" of 1925, an event that has significance for present battles over the public school curriculum. For teachers and students.

Howe, Mark DeWolfe. *The Garden and the Wilderness: Religion and Government in American Constitutional History.* Chicago: University of Chicago Press, 1965.

An argument for what the author terms the "evangelical theory of separation" (as opposed to the Jeffersonian view) as the primary impetus behind the adoption of the religion clauses of the First Amendment. In Howe's view, the First Amendment does not mean neutrality between religion and non-religion or that all aid to religion is unconstitutional. For teachers.

Menendez, Albert J. *Church-State Relations: An Annotated Bibliography.* New York: Garland Publishing, Inc., 1976.

A valuable guide to books on church-state relations. Though the entries are primarily concerned with the United States, there is a representative sample of books dealing with other nations. An excellent resource for teachers and students.

— — — . *School Prayer and Other Religious Issues in American Public Education: A Bibliography.* New York: Garland Publishing, Inc., 1985.

An up-to-date listing of books and articles on religion and education in America. All of the controversies involving the role of religion in public schools from prayer to religious garb in the classroom are included. A helpful tool for students and teachers doing research in this area.

Miller, Robert T. and Ronald B. Flowers. *Toward Benevolent Neutrality: Church, State, and the Supreme Court.* Waco: Markham Press Fund, 1985.

This volume contains the Supreme Court decisions given in forty-four cases concerning the religion clauses of the First Amendment. The sections of the book are arranged topically and include brief historical overviews of the cases under consideration. A valuable reference tool for students and teachers.

Pfeffer, Leo. *Church, State, and Freedom.* Rev. ed. Boston: Beacon Press, 1967.

A comprehensive study of the origin and meaning of the religion clauses of the First Amendment. For teachers and students.

— — — . *Religion, State, and the Burger Court.* Buffalo: Prometheus Books, 1985.

This recent book is an excellent discussion of the church-state issues considered by the Burger Court. For teachers and students.

Reichley, James A. *Religion in American Public Life.* Washington, D.C.: The Brookings Institution, 1985.

A provocative discussion of the role churches have played in American political life. Helpful for understanding the current debate about the mixing of religion and politics, a key church-state issue. For teachers.

Stokes, Anson Phelps and Leo Pfeffer. *Church and State in the United States.* New York: Harper and Brothers, 1964.

This is a revised one-volume edition of Stokes' classic work on the relationship of church and state in the United States. An excellent resource for understanding religious influences in American history. For teachers and students.

Warsaw, Thayer S. *Religion, Education, and the Supreme Court.* Nashville: Abingdon, 1979.

A concise, clear examination of what the Supreme Court has said about what is and what is not permitted in schools concerning religion. For teachers and students.

Wood, James F., Jr. ed. *Religion, the State, and Education.* Waco: Baylor University Press, 1985.

Nine recent articles on the role of religion in public education. Recommended for teachers interested in exploring ways to integrate teaching about religion into the curriculum.

— — — ed. *Religion and the State: Essays in Honor of Leo Pfeffer.* Waco: Baylor University Press, 1985.

An outstanding collection of twenty-one original essays on religion and the state. Special attention is given to the meaning of the religion clauses of the First Amendment in contemporary America. Recommended as a valuable resource for teachers and students.

APPENDIX A

Publishers And Distributors

Addision-Wesley
  Publishing Company
2725 Sand Hill Road
Menlo Park, California 94025
(800) 447-2244

American Bar Association
750 North Lake Shore Drive
Chicago, Illinois 60611
(312) 988-5733

Anti-Defamation League
823 United Nations Plaza
New York, New York 10017
(212) 490-2525

Barr Films
P.O. Box 5667
3490 East Foothill Boulevard
Pasadena, California 91107
(818) 793-6153

Bauman Bible Telecasts
3436 Lee Highway, #200
Arlington, VA 22207
(703) 243-1300

Close Up Foundation
1235 Jefferson Davis Highway
Suite 1500
Arlington, Virginia 22202
(703) 892-5400

Constitutional Rights Foundation
1510 Cotner Avenue
Los Angeles, California 90025
(213) 487-5590

Coronet/MTI
108 Wilmot Road
Deerfield, Illinois 60015
(800) 621-2131
In Illinois and Alaska call collect
(312) 940-1260

Council for the Advancement
  of Citizenship
One Dupont Circle, Suite 520
Washington, D.C. 20036
(202) 861-2583

Encyclopaedia Britannica
  Corporation
Preview and Rental Department
425 North Michigan Avenue
10th Floor
Chicago, Illinois 60645
(312) 347-7000

McGraw-Hill
P.O. Box 641
Del Mar, California 92014
(619) 453-5000

National Textbook Company
8259 Niles Center Road
Skokie, Illinois 60076
(312) 679-5500

Phoenix Films & Video, Inc.
468 Park Avenue, South
New York, NY 10016
(212) 684-5910

Random House School Division
Department 9050
400 Hahn Road
Westminster, MD 2157
(800) 638-6460
In Maryland call toll free
(800) 492-0782
In Alaska and Hawaii call collect
(301) 848-1900

Social Issues Resources
  Series, Inc. (SIRS)
P.O. Box 2507
Boca Raton, Florida 33427
(800) 327-0513
In Florida, Alaska and Hawaii call
(305) 994-0079

Social Studies School Service
10,000 Culver Boulevard, Room 1
P.O. Box 802
Culver City, California 90232
(800) 421-4246
In California call (213) 839-2436

Virginia Department of Education
P.O. Box 6-Q
Richmond, VA 23216-2060
(804) 225-2398

West Publishing Company
50 West Kellogg Blvd.
P.O. Box 64526
St. Paul, Minnesota 55164-0526
(800) 328-9352
In Minnesota call (612) 228-2973

APPENDIX B

FIELD TRIP SITES

Listed below are a number of significant places connected with the birth of religious freedom in the United States.

Maryland

Freedom of Conscience Monument,
Near St. Mary's College

Erected to commemorate the passage of the Act Concerning Religion (now known as the Toleration Act) in 1649. In an age of religious persecution and intolerance, this act granted an unusual degree of religious liberty to all Christians.

For more information about this and other historical sites in Maryland, contact the Maryland Archives, P.O. Box 828, Annapolis, MD 21404. They have a number of helpful publications including two pamphlets on religious freedom in Maryland.

Massachusetts

Plymouth Rock, Plymouth

The Pilgrims arrived at this spot in 1620 seeking freedom of worship. Today's Plymouth offers a re-creation of Pilgrim life at Plimouth Plantation, a museum, and a replica of the Mayflower.

Black Heritage Trail, Boston

The story of Black religious life in America is inseparable from the struggle of Black Americans for freedom and equality. The Black Heritage Trail includes the Old African Meeting House, the oldest Black church building (1805) still standing in the United States. The trail also includes visits to a number of important sites connected with the abolitionist movement.

Salem Witchcraft Trials, Salem

The tragic witchcraft trials of the 17th century are remembered in an audio-visual re-creation at the Salem Witch Museum and a live reenactment at the Witch Dungeon Museum.

103

Massachusetts, as the home of the Puritans, was an important battleground in the struggle for religious liberty. For more information about places to see in Boston and throughout the state, contact: The Spirit of Massachusetts, Division of Tourism, 100 Cambridge Street, 13th Floor, Boston, MA 02202

Pennsylvania

William Penn Memorial Museum, Harrisburg

William Penn was one of the earliest champions of religious freedom. This museum contains, among other items, the original charter given to Penn by King Charles II.

Independence National Historical Park,
Philadelphia

Pennsylvania was Penn's "Holy Experiment" in freedom of religion. Consequently, many sites in the "City of Brotherly Love" are connected with the story of religious freedom in America.

For pamphlets and maps describing places to see in Pennsylvania, write: Bureau of Travel Development, Pennsylvania Department of Commerce, 416 Forum Building, Harrisburg, PA 17120

Rhode Island

Roger Williams National Memorial,
Providence

Roger Williams founded Rhode Island in 1636 as a place where all people could enjoy full freedom of religion. The colony became a haven for Jews, Quakers and others unwelcome elsewhere.

This memorial is a park and information center located on the site of the original settlement. Providence also has the Williams Memorial Monument, a large statue of the founder gazing out over the city. Throughout the city there are reminders of Williams' legacy of freedom.

For more information and a guide to Rhode Island contact: Rhode Island Tourism Division, 7 Jackson Walkway, Providence, RI 02903.

Virginia

The James Madison Museum, Orange

James Madison, the Father of the U.S. Constitution, played a central role in the effort to secure religious liberty for Virginia and the nation. This museum is located in Madison's home county of Orange. The original Orange County Courthouse (no longer standing) was where, in 1768, Separate Baptists were tried for "preaching Schismatick Doctrines." Montpelier, near Orange, was Madison's home for 75 years. It will be open to the public in 1987.

Monticello, Charlottesville

The story of religious freedom in America could not be told without reference to one of its key players, Thomas Jefferson, author of Virginia's famous Bill for Establishing Religious Freedom. Monticello is the magnificent home designed by Jefferson. Here the visitor can get some appreciation for the genius of the man who did so much to create the "wall of separation" between church and state.

Virginia is also known for its historic churches, many of which played an important role in American history. For information about these places and other Virginia attractions, write: Virginia Division of Tourism, 202 North Ninth Street, Richmond, VA 23219.

APPENDIX C

Organizations To Contact

The following organizations can be of assistance to educators interested in teaching about religious freedom.

American Bar Association Special Committee of Youth Education for Citizenship
Charlotte C. Anderson, Staff Director
Minna S. Novick, Bicentennial Project Coordinator
750 N. Lake Shore Drive
Chicago, IL 60611
(312) 988-5725

The ABA Special Committee of Youth Education for Citizenship was established in 1971 as a clearinghouse and coordinator for law-related education. YEFC publishes *Update on Law Related Education* (reviewed in Chapter 5), curriculum catalogs, and other materials. YEFC also offers conferences, summer institutes and consulting services.

Americans United Research Foundation
Robert L. Maddox, Executive Director
900 Silver Spring Avenue
Silver Spring, MD 20910
(301) 588-2282

Americans United sponsors research in various problems involving church-state relations. The Foundation maintains an extensive archives containing materials related to religious freedom issues.

Anti-Defamation League of B'nai B'rith
Frances M. Sonnenschein, Director Education Dept.
823 United Nations Plaza
New York, NY 10017
(212) 490-2525

The Anti-Defamation League produces excellent human relations materials for teachers that supply accurate information about racial and ethnic minorities. Write for their free catalogue.

National Archives and Records Administration
Elsie T. Freeman, Chief, Education Branch
Office of Public Programs
National Archives Washington, D.C. 20408
(202) 523-3298

The National Archives is responsible for the preservation and use of the permanently valuable records of the federal government. Teachers and students are welcome to use their research facilities in Washington, D.C. and in branch offices across the nation. The Archives develops teaching materials, conducts workshops in the use of primary sources in the classroom, and offers courses in research methods.

National Council on Religion and Public Education

Lynn Taylor, Executive Director
1300 Oread Avenue
Lawrence, KS 66045
(913) 843-7257

The NCRPE is a coalition of organizations concerned with the study of religion in public education. Its central purpose is "to provide a forum and means for cooperation among organizations and institutions concerned with those ways of studying religion which are educationally appropriate and constitutionally acceptable to a secular program of public education." The NCRPE will provide teachers with information about curriculum materials, teacher education opportunities, and programs related to religion and public education.

About the Author

Charles C. Haynes is a Research Associate for Americans United Research Foundation. He has a Master's degree in religion and education from Harvard Divinity School and a Doctorate in theological studies from Emory University. He formerly taught religion at Randolph-Macon College where he served as Director of Religious Life. Dr. Haynes has also taught social studies in both public and private secondary schools.

Americans United Research Foundation

Americans United Research Foundation was formed in 1969 to sponsor research and education about freedom of religion. Since its founding, the Foundation has published a number of significant studies concerning church-state and other religious liberty issues. Americans United maintains an extensive archives and offers internship opportunities annually to college students. This publication is part of the Foundation's Teach Religious Freedom Project, an ongoing effort to promote education about our first freedom.